# THE POWER OF

Joy
and
PURPOSE

# THE POWER OF

# PURPOSE

## 7 PRESENCE PRINCIPLES AND TOOLS

### NICOLE MARTIN

Publisher:
Nicole Martin
HRBoost, LLC.
*www.hrboost.com*
847-282-4038

Publishing consultant:
Professional Woman Publishing, LLC
*www.pwnbooks.com*

ISBN: 978-0-578-20760-5

*This book is truly dedicated
to all God loving people.*

# Contents

# Preface

Everyone deserves to feel joy and purpose each and every day. Every human seeks to find a deeper meaning in what they do, how they live, why they are here. Yet many are still searching. There is no perfect time to find answers to our deepest questions. I have found the answers are often right before you, already deep within you, waiting to be exposed. The question is, are you ready to begin your journey to who you really were meant to be? People will say we should feel content and blessed with what we have versus what we do not have. Yet, many will look externally to gauge how they are doing. How do I look in the mirror? Is my home spacious and inviting? Do I drive a luxury car or have I taken an exotic trip? But do you truly wake up embracing each day with joy? If you do, from what do you source your joy? With 20 extra pounds on your hips and expression lines on your face, are you capable of looking in the mirror and see the beauty that radiates from within you? Do you jump out of bed with a purpose that truly fulfills you? I do not know the exact moment I began to breathe with contentment in my heart. Maybe I always had a touch of gratitude in my being or maybe my mother just had a way of keeping me grounded. As a teenager growing up in a small railroad town in Montana, I can remember the day I was just casually browsing through one of my mother's *Reader's Digest* magazines when I read my favorite quote. To this day, it is "Presence is more than just being Present." The quote has never left me; it remains a most significant and guiding inspiration. But what is *presence*? Some may call it a combination of self-assertion and a desire for inclusiveness. If you were to define presence you would simply state that presence is the state or fact of existing, occurring, or being present in a place or thing. Some would argue that presence is simply one that is present, such as the actual person or thing that is present, essentially, something present of a visible or concrete nature. The word can even denote the air of a person, especially one of a stately or distinguished bearing setting forth a noteworthy quality of poise and effectiveness. I would tend to regard *presence* as something else. *Presence truly* is so much more than being present. Just as the quote sets forth, *presence* can be felt in a tangible way but I would argue that must come from something intangible. For me, *presence* is derived from a deep awareness of soul and Spirit. We can all identify with self but do you believe in soul and Spirit? Do you identify with Spirit? Spirit is the nonphysical part of a person that is the seat of emotions and character; your life force. Your first breath and your last breath are set forth by Spirit. Presence can be realized when self is in full presence and awareness of the soul and the Spirit, ultimately seeking harmony between body and Spirit. Today, I live with presence in my daily practice, and it has brought me to a deeper place of gratitude moment to moment. Was I always like this? No.

Many who have come to know me have remarked that I am a driven individual. I do not see myself as driven but rather purposeful. I have a craving to know more, to learn more and never be cured of my curiosity. I feel presence is an awareness of every grace I have been granted by God. I have come to living in the present moment with a sense of power and strength. This awareness I feel propels me to live presence from wherever I stand. Do not confuse presence with an outward expression, as it is not an outward expression. It is sourced from our inner thoughts and feelings and then ideally lived outward in the form of love. Every life experiences struggle. How we move through these struggles either destroys our sense of joy for life or it deepens us to emerge with a compassionate heart and a truer desire to live in harmony to the good of God and all living things.

The private things we speak to ourselves are truly the embers that fuel presence. Psychologist and researcher Dr. Albert Ellis created the ABC model to help us understand the meaning of our reactions to adversity: "A" is the adversity—the situation or event. "B" is our belief—our explanation about why the situation happened. "C" is the consequence—the feelings and behaviors that our belief causes. In thinking of this simple equation, visualize "A" + "B" = "C." We all experience "A," whatever "A" might be. Yet many feel "B" is put upon them rather than "A." "A" is put upon them. We all have the ability to claim the personal power to choose "B." By doing so, we each have the choice to effectively change the outcome in "C." We always have the personal power to choose "C." We can choose to be joyful, peaceful, loving, even forgiving, once we become aware of this personal power and choice. By choosing to be more present, I realize it can change life for the better by bringing you closer to your true purpose and calling by looking deeper into each moment for not what is at the surface but the opportunity before you. By choosing to not react quickly but to think, reflect, and then project presence, you can realize the opportunities before you.

I did not always possess this grace. Self-awareness and presence is a daily practice. I cannot say that I always loved myself. I cannot say that I always forgave so easily. I do not know that I ever saw myself as a survivor. I was not always empowered and I certainly did not feel a keen sense of esteem. Ironically, I just met a new connection during what I call a "meet and greet." Not long after we exchanged, he chuckled and proclaimed, "Nicole, you have a keen sense of self-esteem." I thought to myself, well shouldn't we all? I questioned back, "Do you mean confidence?" He reaffirmed, "No, esteem. It's a good thing." Days later, I find myself amazed by the effect my presence has on others. Often, when I meet people, they will comment on my "energy" or my "presence." It has been decades of interactions with others that have led me to proclaim the power of presence. We all have presence. The opportunity is to engage your presence in a meaningful way. I think of this often, not aloud, but in my most private thoughts. I reflect and self-correct to question if I was truly present in any given moment. Be it with a person or a moment to myself. Was I absent of all distraction? In fact, I often gain knowledge in retrospect, and in moments where I may have slipped from presence and become merely present, I learn. To reflect and learn has been my saving grace. I have overcome fear, been kind to myself in laughter and in sadness, and I feel I can embrace each day with a willingness to accept what may come ... knowing all is as it should be.

*Joy!* When was the last time you felt genuine *joy?* Joy is generally a feeling of great happiness. I live joy as a deeply satisfying sense of the present whereby I choose to be joyful. Choice is very important. Example: This morning I had several tasks to accomplish before I could sit down and write. While I was working at my desk, my young son was at my feet, "Mama, Mama, Mama!" meanwhile my love was not far off in the kitchen, and he was complaining about something I left out on the counter. I was just trying to focus on my task in the office. Instead of becoming irritated, I chose to breathe, get up, pick up my little guy, breathe in his sweet baby scent and make my way to my husband. I affirm him, I hear him, I apologize and restate what I must do to accomplish my tasks and I return to task with *presence*. Many delays impeded my morning and I am about 5 hours behind schedule today. Yet, that was all "A." I choose to embrace "A" by claiming *presence* in the gracious moment I have now. This moment. With you that is "B." Where I dedicate my *presence* now will lead to "C." "C" will be me sharing, openly, candidly in the hope that something I have lived through will inspire you to live through it too. Not just to get through it, but to live it, to feel it, to breathe it, to enjoy it, and to fuel it with purpose.

Purpose is the reason for which something is done or created, or for which something exists. I live purpose as my intent to serve a divinity higher than myself. It is with *joy* and purpose that I approach each day. I have had to learn to love myself, forgive many, and overcome fear. Only after we truly get to know ourselves and embrace who we are can we see the blessings we have been bestowed. This journey is for each of us and it is lifelong. Through my journey thus far, I have found a lens of love. Love that fills my heart to such a degree that it is bursting with *joy!* It is with this *joy* that I am fueled with purpose to share. If you feel as if your life is not your own, then this book will help you. You deserve to transform your anxiety and fear into personal power, *joy* and peace of mind. This book is about the choices we make every single day and how those choices can guide you to come into your own authentic self, ultimately sourcing joy and purpose from within, and propelling you forward to feel peace, power and *joy!*

# Acknowledgements

It is difficult to name all those for whom I am grateful. It seems appropriate to begin with my mother. Through the grace of God, she brought me into this world at a tender age. She was nineteen and together we grew as she shaped me into the adult I have become. It wasn't until I began writing this book that I had the epiphany that this book should be written in collaboration with my mother. She always has listened and with wisdom that never fails, she helps me see the bigger picture and make sense of my fears and pain. Sometimes directly and sometimes indirectly, she has taught me to hear my own voice and to *always* believe in it. I pointed much of my gratitude to God, but as I began to write, it became evident that I began to share tools I learned long ago. Perhaps my heart has always known. I have a friend whom I met when he was in seminary, and he has since become a priest. I carry with me something he once said to me: "Su corazón conoce al Señor y eso es suficiente" which translates to "... her heart knows the Lord and that is enough."

*The Power of Joy and Purpose* is something that is undeniable to me and I am hopeful that by sharing my story it can lift the spirits of many. In a way, this entire book is a gesture of never-ending love to my mother. The potential to share my experiences, good, bad, ugly, or indifferent, is to acknowledge that I have moved through, grown from, and enriched my life moment to moment. We all make choices. Who we surround ourselves with, look to, and share energy with is critical to how we feel daily. I thank Suzan Quinn Mayworm, whose guidance and friendship has helped me to feel worthy of more. I have found you only need one person who looks at you, sees you, and encourages you to see yourself in loving eyes again and again and again. Unconditional love is truly something I have been blessed to feel and experience.

For my love, Brian Martin, who lovingly devotes his life to our family and our marriage. As we co-create our journey, I feel boundless support and love, and thank him for loving me just as I am. Our beautiful children bring us both tremendous joy and deepen our faith in God and one another. I believe my first-born was a catalyst for personal growth I never imagined, and his birth filled me with overwhelming gratitude. My second-born son has put greater purpose in my life and the inspiration to share joy more openly. To witness their journey as a mother is my greatest gift.

I thank the many beautiful people by which I have learned, be it beside them, with them, or from them. I am eternally grateful for the healers in my life. I thank all those who have given to me and in turn have allowed me to give. I have beautiful souls who grace my life with their *presence*. I am grateful for all of them, those who were brief in time and those who are constants and life-giving. You know who you are and that is all that truly matters.

Graciously,

# PRESENCE PRINCIPLE 1
## *What defines you?*

*"You may encounter many defeats, but you must not be defeated. In fact, it may be necessary to encounter the defeats, so you can know who you are, what you can rise from, how you can still come out of it."*

–MAYA ANGELOU

## The Unexpected

It was a Thursday afternoon in southern California. I had shoulder-length blonde hair, many freckles and a sun-kissed olive complexion from fun-filled days playing outdoors. It was approximately 3:30 p.m. and I had just arrived home from school. Back then, I walked everywhere. It was normal to walk to and from school alone. My mother was always gone before I woke up in the morning and I always had a very specific list of tasks to have done for her before her arrival home each evening. I enjoyed the quiet time

1

after school as the house was all mine. By the early age of nine, I had already come to enjoy the peace of a quiet home. Three years earlier, my younger brother had joined our family and became my mother's second-born. I loved playing with him. I used to literally dress him up in my doll's clothes and enjoy my play tea set with a real "guest." But, of course, he was at day care that afternoon when I arrived home. First stop, the refrigerator, of course! After-school snacks were the best and my mother always stocked the freezer with Schwan's® single-serve pizza's. We had a massive round sofa bed that served as our living room couch. It was something I could run and jump on, and often did. It was a beautiful day, sunny and warm despite being mid-January. Only now have I come to expect cold in winter. I was enjoyed my free time when I should have already begun my chores when the phone rang. It was my mom! She was in a rush and just explained that a client she had worked on the night prior would be stopping by to pick up his wallet. She went on to explain that "Joey" thinks he must have lost it and she asked me to check around the sofa. She specifically gave me permission and instruction to let him into the home and to expect him to come by soon. My mother had worked out of the house for as long as I could remember. She was a certified holistic health practitioner (HHP) and natural energy healer but, as a single mother, had other jobs as well to help support me and my brother. I hung up the phone and began searching as she had asked me to. Ten or fifteen minutes had to have gone by when I heard a knock on the door. It was Joey. He was in his thirties, stood nearly 6' and had blond curly hair. He had broad shoulders, and I remember he was wearing jeans and a light tan canvas jacket. I greeted him and welcomed him in. I began explaining that mom had asked me to look for his wallet but it was nowhere to be found. I walked him into the living room, pointed to all the places I looked and finally apologized and sat down on the round sofa bed in the corner. He approached and sat down next me, and before I knew it he leaned over and began kissing me. I remember he paused and I wiped my mouth with my hand and exclaimed, "Ugh! Why did you do that?" I was so confused. Things progressed quickly as he lifted me off my feet and carried me to the bathroom. I just went along with his demands. My mind was racing and I simply could not make sense of what he was doing. By the grace of God, he was having diffi-culty. I was after all, a young girl. I just went on talking, "What are you doing?" Before I knew it, he picked me up again and took me to my mother's bedroom. He sat on the bed and by this time I was naked. I remember feeling bad for being in my mother's room and just as I glanced right to see the alarm clock, it read 5:12 p.m. I realized in stunning fear that my mother would be home any minute. I became frenzied and frantically telling Joey, "My mom is going to be home any minute and I have to clean this place up. My chores aren't done! I won't tell her what happened, just go, just go, you must leave!" He looked at the clock and ordered me to my knees. He was very forceful with me and before I knew it there was mess everywhere! He looked at me, said, "Sorry!" and left. I was perplexed and had no idea what just happened. I was fearful of the mess that had been made and what my mother would say when she found out my chores weren't done. My heart was racing. I was out of breath and I felt enough adrenalin to dress myself and run out the front door. We lived in a condo well up on a foothill, and there were evergreen hedges that bordered every window and sidewalk in the complex. As I dressed hurriedly, I knew I was going to find help. I was terrified but hadn't shed a tear. I simply was panic-stricken. I estimated it had been one minute since he left. It felt like five. I inched the door open and saw no one. I took a frightful step outside and looked both ways. The only way down to the road were double-width staircases placed every two con-dominiums. I remember thinking he must have gone down the stairs as I heard his voice below. I dropped to my knees on the sidewalk adjacent to the front door of my house. Just steps from the door, I peered beneath the bushes and I could see a taxi on the street below. He hopped in the cab that appeared to be waiting, and I watched the taxi drive away. The minute they were gone and without thinking, I ran to the neighbor's house. I don't remember their names. I simply told them I had been attacked and the rest is history. By the time my mother arrived home, the area had been completely cordoned off. I remember just being relieved that she wasn't mad at me. I recall the shock on her face and the tension in the police car. The policeman who took me in for a statement and examination allowed me to sit in the front seat. I gave my statement with my mother likely watching, but I remember she wasn't in the room. It was easier to tell my story without her next to me. It seems the police knew this. We didn't go home that night and ironically, I don't remember where we slept. I vividly remember my mother sitting me down to let me know the police had located Joey before the next morning. My mother explained that he was charged with hurting many girls, not just me. She explained that I would have to tell my story in a court house and by doing so I would ensure he gets the help he needs and he won't be allowed to hurt another girl. She encouraged me to speak every word of truth and to feel it. She explained that what I feel, I can heal. My mother prayed with me. She explained how I could take my power back and breathe positive energy into the memory. She took the time to not have one conversation that was 60 minutes but rather 60 conversations that were one minute. Are you okay? Do you want to talk about it? What do you want to do to feel happy right now? Are you ready to go back to school? Do you need some time alone? I remember a longer conversation when she asked me if I wanted to talk to someone other than her. I declined and I respect my mom to this day for not making me do something I didn't want to do.

Rather, was not ready to do. She always had a way of treating me like an adult even when I was a child, likely something from her days growing up in a broken home with divorced parents.

Days became weeks and it was time to go to court. I showed up at the Santa Barbara court house, and it was a big place. I remember being staged in rooms, prepared in conversation with a woman I did not know. She walked with me, held me back behind a door, and then leaned over and said, "Don't be nervous, just tell the truth." I walked into the room and was presented from the front of the courtroom vs. the rear as we see on television. I sat myself into the witness stand and peered out over the large room. The chair practically enveloped me. I tried to not see Joey but I could see him. He seemed frail and weak in an orange jumpsuit, not intimidating and strong as I had recalled from my exchange with him. I began speaking and, word for word, told my story. I was nine years old. I looked for my mother as I nervously quoted things Joey had said to me. I had never spoken vulgar words before but I replayed it like a movie for all to hear. After it was all said and done, many behind the scenes affirmed to me and let me know how brave and strong I was, and that by telling the truth, my actions in turn had helped many. Upon my return home, my mother prayed with me again and asked me to ask God to see it as I would have preferred it to happen. Aloud, I shared I would have preferred that I had found his wallet and that he would have taken it, said thank you and left. I would have liked to have had my chores done when my mother came home and I wish I didn't feel so confused. I would like to feel safe and be understood. After I said all of that, my mother helped me to send all the blessings I would wish for my assailant. She explained that if I didn't send him blessings in prayer, then the negative emotions I have felt would stay with me when truly I had the power to release them in the form of blessings. She explained I must will it to God to harmonize to the good of all living things.

5

Life returned to normal, whatever that is, and my mother had arranged for me to walk to a friend's house after school. This would be the routine for the remainder of the school year. I remember she was working with me to let go of what happened. Speaking my truth and having my mother support me through my truth helped me heal my fragmented feelings I was feeling. At an early age, she taught me that just because this happened to me (A) it does not need to change who God intended me to be. It will not have power to define me unless I give it that power. Something that I couldn't escape was people knowing about what happened to me where we lived. It was in the papers; my teachers were notified, and I missed school. In the months that followed, I recall it feeling like a fog. A thick cloud of energy seemed to surround me and it simply wouldn't leave. Girls at school would whisper in corners, "... that was the girl who was attacked." I became withdrawn. I equate it to feeling defunct. I recall my mother gifted me a rose-quartz necklace. She asked me to wear it every day until I felt better. Rose-quartz is one of the most popular crystals[1] in healing. Many regard it as a healing crystal for attracting and keeping love. Rose quartz is also used when it comes to healing one's heart from pain and disappointment. Months later, I recall it mysteriously breaking. The gem literally cracked in half from the pendent on my necklace. I told my mother right away and she simply let me know it has done its job. Days turned into weeks and weeks into months. Despite the positive exchanges with prayer, I didn't believe in the true power of the prayer. By summer of the same year I didn't feel physically well. In fact, I began experiencing physical pain. I remember it was the Fourth of July holiday and my mother was yards ahead of me as we walked to see fireworks. I couldn't keep up. I felt fatigued, stiff, weak and truly unable to walk. My mother took me to the hospital. She was stunned when they admitted me. Even more so when I was there for a week and despite many physicians and many tests, they couldn't figure out what was wrong. In the end, I was discharged with a diagnosis of Juvenile Rheumatoid Arthritis (JRA). This is a type of arthritis that causes joint inflammation and stiffness for more than six weeks in a child aged 16 or younger. It affects approximately 50,000 children in the United States. I was still overly fearful about security, and fearful.in general. I was feeling I may not belong anywhere, and it was hard to visualize my dreams. Thus, I was having difficulty letting go and I held onto fear. I had trapped negative energy and despite my mother being a healer, she could not do the healing for me. I had to do the work myself.

During those same months, these events had a significant effect on my mother. She had decided to leave all she had ever known. She was planning to move us out of California to a drier climate as the physicians advised this would help. She took a trip to Montana and fell in love with the Gallatin Gateway. Upon her return and before my school year began, she explained she bought a home in Montana and we were leaving California. It would be a fresh start. I remember the emphasis she placed on this for me specifically. She positioned this move as a wonderful opportunity to go somewhere no one knows you and introduce yourself as only you want to be seen. "Every day is a new day and don't you ever waste a single day," she said, "God put you here for a reason!" She would remind me, "You are not a victim just because people say you are a victim." She made it very clear, not only with her words but her actions. She never placed blame on anyone or anything for what happened to me.

As a result, I ultimately learned God does not punish us and I cannot change what happens. It was ingrained in me to deal with what happens, come what may. I learned something more valuable. I can control how I react to what happens. What do I do with it? Do I give energy and power to the negative or do I give

7

energy and power to the positive? For every difficult and unforeseen event, we are faced with a choice. We can emerge from our circumstance with hostility or benevolence.

I define this; I determine what was taken from me. I chose to claim my personal power, to move through it intimately and to rise from it filled with learning rather than suffering. This is a life-changing principle. I know this now and only now do I know with clarity how pivotal this has become to who I am today.

*Presence Principle* number one is the foundation of what defines you. It is at the core of your being. It may be hard to know all you know about yourself and be able to look in the mirror and not see unresolved pain and hurt masked by rage or fear and even a mask you have created for yourself. I know and love beautiful men and women. Many are still stuck in their past, stuck with "A." If you are one of these beautiful souls who feels pain, sadness, shame, or even hostility, you must take your power back. You must reveal what you have learned and emerge from the experience with wisdom and facts. Let go of the negative energy and feelings. The blessings often can be found in working through the pain to find the healing. If you have a secret, speak your truth. You may not have to declare it to the world but to those most intimate to you. You must speak it aloud. How can you feel the full beauty of divine love if deep down you believe that you are damaged, not worthy or less than? The one who loves you accepts you and loves you, but if you believe that could change if they knew "A," then you have not fully moved through to heal. To lend trust to another human is to have trust in yourself and in the grace that you are not alone. You are not alone in anything.

If you speak your truth and find it falls on deaf ears, then that does not change the fact that you still have a choice. If someone fails to hear your truth, the choice has become theirs. If their choice does not help facilitate acknowledgement of your truth, well then, the choice becomes yours once more. You retain the power; you retain the choice. What you do with it is critical. It defines you; it becomes the energy you carry with you and project to others. Ultimately, it is in those moments that we either give pieces of our Spirit away or strengthen our soul through presence. It is to be seen fully with all your greatest fears exposed, and then to be blessed by another human who takes you by the hand and sees your intrinsic beauty. Know that is a moment every soul can accomplish. To see the battle wounds and yet witness an individual that extends energy with benevolence and grace. If you do the work, commit to yourself to look in the mirror and see eyes of strength. Such strength in personal power lays a radiant foundation for your personal presence. This is work. Anything worth doing is work. By healing our wounds, speaking our truth and allowing ourselves to not be defined by what happens to us, the potential is to ultimately bring you closer to your soul's connection and the truth in your purpose.

## PRESENCE TOOLS 1 - WHAT DEFINES YOU?

# — SKETCH YOUR REFLECTION IN THE MIRROR —

*"All the world is full of suffering; it is also full of overcoming it."*

~HELEN KELLER

Remember, in the preface I set forth the thinking of this simple equation. You may recall it. Work to visualize "A" + "B" = "C." We all experience "A", whatever "A" might be. Yet many feel "B" is put upon them rather than "A." "A" is put upon them. We all could claim the personal power to choose "B." By doing so, we each have the choice to effectively change the outcome in "C." We always have the personal power to choose "C."

## Examples Of "A"

"A" is the "unexpected" that is put upon us. It can be illness, injury, losing someone who has passed on or cut us off, assault, rape, bullying, demeaning statements or anything that is put upon you. If you feel negative emotion, thoughts from it, as small as it may seem, that is "A." It can be something traumatic that you did not experience directly but rather witnessed. You may have just seen it or heard it, but it can still be something you carry.

## Ways "A" Can Manifest In Our Life

The work is worth investing in to heal your Spirit and your soul. Those of us who believe that to be born with "Christ Consciousness" are aware that our soul is imprinted knowing what is right and what is wrong among humanity. Each of us has Spirit. Again, Spirit is your life force. Your Spirit is the first breath you take and the last breath you take. Our Spirit must choose to accept it and work through the negative emotions of guilt, rage, sadness, panic, self-doubt, fear and anxiety. Believe you can overcome adversity to a reach a higher level of compassion and gratitude. To work through the emotion is to allow our Spirit to learn the good, bad and indifferent. To deny forgiveness and truth is to embrace complacency. To go about life without feeling the pain or sorrow means we are stuffing it down, burying it and denying truth.

When we fail to acknowledge "A," it can manifest in negative ways. This negative energy can block your heart from love, diminish your energy and lower your Spirit's vibration. At our core, all we are made up of is energy, and our vibration is simply the movement of our energy through space. Our vibrations are very important because they are responsible for how our lives unfold. Through the Law of Attraction, we create our entire lives based on our vibrations. In simple terms, when we have a high vibration we create more of what we want in life, and when our energy is low, we create more of what we do not want. There are four ways in which "A" (what happens to us through our experiences) can manifest and we allow, consciously or unconsciously, the negative energy of "A" to reside within us. It can be experienced in the form of illness, anxiety, toxicity, fear, fright, and isolation from others. When "A" manifests, it can be felt in many ways:

| Vibration "High" | |
| --- | --- |
| Compassion/Gratitude | Third Eye/Crown Chakra "Pituitary/Hypothalamus" |
| Empathy | Heart Chakra "Heart/Thymus" |
| Sympathy | Solar Plexus Chakra "Stomach/Pancreas" |
| Self-Pity – Pity | Sacral Chakra "Ovaries/Testes" |
| Vibration "Low" | |

**Figure 1** Energy Phases from Pity to Compassion; Manifestations of "A" & Correlating Chakra

The first way energy can be felt is *Self-Pity* – the lowest vibrational level. You sit and wallow in it. Self-pity keeps you as the victim, and it allows "A" to reside within you as a "victim seed," essentially creating pity within you. Self-pity is your own.

*Pity* means feeling sorry for others and carrying their burden when it's not yours. Essentially, pity makes you feel akin to others, and that leads to a deep emotional attachment. Pity has a slightly negative connotation, as it can refer to condescension. If you see a disabled person, you may be filled with pity, and you may start to feel sorry for this person. At other times, you may be moved by the misfortune of an individual and start to pity another person for their bad condition.

The second healing level is *Sympathy.* Sympathy is different – in pity, you feel sorry; in sympathy, you understand another's feelings. Sympathy is a very common human emotion. It shows others that you're there for them and share their feelings. For example, if someone is experiencing challenging times, you can sympathize and share how you understand the grief, sorrow, or distress. When someone passes away, we offer sympathy to provide support to our friends in their time of grief and sorrow.

The healing third level begins with *Empathy.* Empathy goes a step further than sympathy, when you choose to reside with the pain of others. Essentially, it's unhealthy when your emotions become confused with other people's, and those feelings become your own unnecessarily. However, to feel pain in empathy and then move through it to compassion is a progression of healing.

When we feel empathy at an unhealthy level, we end up wallowing in the "mud puddle" with that person. When we are in empathy, we are seeing it and feeling it. When someone shares their story with you and you hold onto the pain through empathy, this does not raise energy to compassion and gratitude.

The higher fourth level is *Compassion*. Negative energy can be put on you. But if you're conscious of your power to process the facts of "A," you can choose to lift your Spirit out of the negative energy. You have the personal power within you, and you can choose to move through the emotions, feel them, and then carry them to a place of compassion. To walk with compassion in your heart is to free yourself from the emotion. By choosing to move forward with the lesson for your soul, "A" can become accountable to your Spirit for the balance of the love your soul deserves.

At any given time, we are all on a spectrum that ranges from emotions of hate all the way to the polarity that is unconditional love. This is present with all things. How we see "A" is critical to how we move toward unconditional love. With unconditional love, we reach gratitude, and an unclouded vision becomes apparent as the highest level of vibrational energy is reached.

The first step is to take the time to document and make a full personal inventory of what "A" is to you. Work from birth to the current day. Begin with the worst or most critical thought or incident that comes to mind. All your thoughts, emotions, memories, and experiences reside within you. Some will be easy to recall, others take time, and still others are not with the conscious – your subconscious carries them. Some of us have blocked energy and may not recall memories from birth. In that case, work backward from now. Use this personal inventory worksheet to list everything negative that you may be carrying with you. We will work through this when we get to the *Presence Principle* in the next chapter.

You must love yourself enough to believe that you're worthy to find the happiness you deserve. You must look with eyes of faith to what is before you. Trust in the blessings. Start with the most prominent thoughts that occupy your mind with suffering, then give yourself enough time to uncover the source of suffering and the blessing in your challenge. Focus on the spiritual quality that

14

is allowing you to make connections. As you revisit your memories and experiences, imagine being surrounded and protected by God's love. It is always there for you; you need only ask for the protection.

## PRESENCE TOOLS 1 - WHAT DEFINES YOU?
——— PERSONAL INVENTORY OF "A" ———

| Example Of A | Your Notes |
|---|---|
| Birth Family (Experiences) | |
| Friends (From Past or Present) | |
| Medical (Illness, Surgeries) | |
| Injury (Accidents, Rehab) | |
| Trauma (Of any kind ...) | |
| Abuse (Verbal, Physical, Sexual) | |
| Other: | |

# *Find the Happiness You Deserve*

*"We don't see things as they are. We see things as we are."*

–ANAÏS NIN

## Letting Go

We all grow up. For many, it is journey with distinct milestones along the way. Many recall their 18th birthday as a rite of passage. I remember feeling sad on my 18th birthday. Maybe it was because I was raised to always know I would have to work to put a roof over my head, and I began to feel the weight of greater responsibilities coming my way. I had grown into a young woman and just as my mother had hoped, I was eager to see beyond the small town we lived in. She never intended for me to stay close to home. She simply had hoped to create a safe environment for me to grow and develop, free of fear and judgments or restrictions set forth by city truths. Today, I often get asked how I ever left a place as beautiful as Montana. It is an easy reply: "The first thing you want to do when you grow up in small town is leave. The ironic thing is when you learn enough, you find that you want to go back." Despite my accomplishments in high school, I was never aiming for college. Oddly, my mother never placed those expectations on me nor did it seem like a natural next step. Many graduate high school in Montana and go into trades. Others settle down early in life, and I simply knew I wasn't doing either of those things. I knew I wanted to work and with striking independence at an early age, I ventured across the country and as I look back to that day, it was the day after high school graduation that I packed up my little Nissan with everything I owned and headed east to Chicago. A sharp contrast to life in Montana, I recall it feeling like culture shock. I remember my naiveté. I had never seen a parking garage, let alone a skyscraper and it seemed everyone was so dressed up. I had taken up residence with my godmother's family. A trusted friend of my mother, my godmother welcomed me into her home. Having known her my entire life, it seemed I was with family despite being 1,300 miles from home. I was fortunate to have a job offer before I graduated high school and going straight to work in the big city was like a dream. Could I have gone on to university? Absolutely! It simply was not put before me at the time. Knowing I would pay my own way, a job was my core focus. I was thrilled to be earning my own money and I was even more excited to afford my own place. I had my first apartment within six months.

I was loving life. Being young and free, it wasn't long before I had a network of new friends. One of my friends had invited me to a dairy farm in Wisconsin for a weekend. It so reminded of Montana. Sure, the mountains were missing but the people were friendly and affable. The pace of life was more relaxed and the beauty of the landscape was so reminiscent of home. I found myself truly grateful to go along. I was not seeking nor was I expecting to fall in love. But there he was, a very attractive man in his rugged blue jeans, flannel shirt and a cap. Quite good-looking and looking back, it seems he looked like every man I saw growing up back home in Montana. He came in for dinner with the family. He had such a lovely smile and an enthusiastic sense of humor. My friend was his sister and she noticed we had chemistry. As the weekend continued, she did not think much of our exchanges at first. In fact, neither did I. As Sunday arrived, we began packing to make our return to Chicago. Moments before we left, he pulled me aside and gave me his number and extended an open invitation to come again sometime. Needless to say, I found my way to Wisconsin weekend after weekend. I recall my godmother asking, "Why do you always make the trip to him? He should make the trip to you!" For a full year, we had a long-distance relationship. I didn't mind it one bit. I had found a school I could afford, so I elected to take some courses part-time. The classes at the local community college along with work had kept me quite busy. I simply enjoyed our relationship and no expectations of the future. I was very focused on my personal goals. He had more serious intentions, I came to find. As the second year approached, he moved back to Illinois and took up his family's' trade, general contracting homes. We had great plans, even designing a home together. In his off-time, he was devoting his time to building "our home" and it seemed natural to dream of "our life" in the future. I invited him to visit Montana with me during my annual visit to my mother. I remember the trip was joyful for us both. He seemed to get along well with all of my friends and family. Our life was making all the natural progressions. I absolutely loved his family (maybe too much, in fact) and we often spent time with them. He came from a large family, one of five children, and I simply loved them all. Looking back, I may have loved his family as much if not more than him.

That same year was coming to an end and I had planned a second trip back to Montana for the holidays alone. It was a crazy time, as I was taking six courses or 18 credit hours and working full-time. I missed my mom and I was eager to make the trip despite having just moved into our new home. My heart was lonely, it seemed, but I didn't connect it to my relationship. I instead thought I was homesick. I recall arriving from this trip to Montana and for the first time in my life, it did not feel like home. Oddly, it felt like I was a visitor in the home I grew up in, and it was one of the oddest realities. I lived in an entirely new place and was building a home of my own with someone else. My mother's home always feels like home to me, but this trip it became clear to me that her home was not my home. I had built a new life across the country and it had greater prominence in my life. To my surprise, I did not know if or when I would return to Montana.

I have a brother seven years younger and at the time I was 20 years old. He had just turned 13 years old and was mid-year into the 7th grade as it was January. My mother had shared with me how he was getting into trouble, and she seemed to be arguing with my step-father at the time. I grew up without a father and my mother married when I was 15 but I was nearly grown. My loyalties lay with my mother. Surprisingly, I arrived this holiday to witness a changed environment. My mother seemed concerned for my brother and there appeared to be tensions between my mother and step-father. I simply didn't see a positive environment for my brother. There is nothing to do in a small town. When I was young, I worked and was overly involved in school and extra-curricular activities. All I could see when I looked at my younger brother was the lack of a strong father figure in his life. I pondered if he just needed to see how much opportunity there really was outside of the small town he lived in. My very early years were in California so I had a different lens. My young brother had only ever recalled his life in Montana. It seemed to be he had feelings of hopelessness. You get into trouble in a small town and you are always regarded as such. As a result, he questioned if he could ever overcome the erroneous reputation by affiliation. I found myself thinking I needed to take him out of the small town we grew up in. An impulsive thought at the time, but I simply knew I could fix it. I had a home with an extra room. I lived in a community with excellent schools. Without hesitation, I looked at my mother and proposed he come home with me. She could see I was serious. I don't recall my brother being given a choice in the matter, but he had no hesitation in coming back to Illinois with me. I don't even recall calling my boyfriend and asking him. I had made the decision in a moment of clarity and never looked back. It was simple. It was the right thing to do.

We traveled back to Illinois and the transition was seamless. My brother continued his 7th grade year in Illinois and I remember thinking how my boyfriend was a good role model for him, and perhaps living with us would afford him a second chance of sorts; a way to begin new and start fresh similar to what I experienced as a young girl. He assimilated very well and began to be more joyful. He solidified his relationship with my boyfriend and his family. I had essentially taken guardianship of my younger brother and at 20 years of age, I was attending his parent/teacher conferences. Within four months, my boyfriend asked me to marry him. I remember saying, "YES!" with such *joy* in my heart and rushed over to my godmother's home on my way to work to share the news. She was amazed and surprised, but as always, kind and loving. She simply asked, "Is this really what you want? You're still going to school and you are so young." I exclaimed, "Oh yes!" Wedding planning began straightaway and I was fully engulfed with work, school, mothering my young brother, etc. I had never even been out to a dance club, never obtained a degree, never traveled beyond our shores. I was not yet 21. I seemed to be running through the motions of what seemed reasonable. We had been together for two years. Marriage seemed a reasonable next step.

In a moment, it all changed. I was at work. It was morning and I recall standing at the reception desk at the company I worked at and peering out the window. I could see my sporty Toyota Celica being pulled away by a tow truck. I was stunned, horrified in fact. What was happening? I said something aloud to a co-worker nearby and she said, "Call your bank!" Of course, I immediately did. I was thinking of my legal rights and how could they, and then I heard it on the other end of the phone, "Ma'am, we have not received your car payments in two months! Your car is being repossessed." I was confused, shocked, and unclear. How could that be? I had given all of my payments to my fiancé and he took care to send them as I was so busy between school and work. This was in the days before online bill pay and I simply delegated my bill paying to him. I found myself suddenly upset. I couldn't work, and I needed answers. I excused myself from work and rushed straight home. My fiancé was not there as I had expected. Our house was his project after all. Where was he? I called his best friend's house. The wife explained that the men had gone fishing.

Fishing? I thought to myself, "... in the middle of the week on a work day?" I never assumed that he wasn't working when I was working. Something seemed off. My heart was racing. I drove straight there. What I found were two men drinking, drunk in fact. As I questioned and demanded answers, the truth was revealed. He had taken the money I had entrusted him to pay bills with and he bought my engagement ring with the money. There are no words to express my horror. I was absolutely beyond words. I felt so betrayed and as the story goes, it got worse. We went home and as I looked around, I found hidden cases of beer. It was as if I had pulled the blinds back for the very first time. It was suddenly all so clear. I searched symptoms online for closet alcoholics or high-functioning alcohol abuse. I was engaged to a closet alcoholic. I had excused a few of the symptoms as I knew he had survivor's guilt. He was a sole surviving twin. My immediate thought was not to leave him, but rather it was to help him. I mentally made a commitment to be by his side and walk with him as he confronted his addiction.

Ironically, having my young brother with me made me stronger in the weeks that followed. I was more present in every moment. Prior, I had allowed myself to very distracted. It was easy to have my mind on work or school. I found myself holding stronger to my convictions. Imagine someone saying something rude to you. You might quip back and move on only for it to happen again in a few days or weeks, again and again. However, with the responsibility I had for my brother, I analyzed everything ten times greater. Something that may have otherwise been overlooked suddenly held great meaning. I sat down with my fiancé and we came to an agreement. I expected him to go to AA meetings and get help. I was close with his mother at the time and I revealed all to her and I asked her for support. I had no plan, no money, and no solutions. We would work through this together. Within weeks, he had broken our agreement just as I knew he would. It was then it became clear. I had to leave. I told him I was done. He was enraged. I grabbed my brother, his school bag and my purse and we ran to the car. I will never forget how his fist hit the driver's side window as I reversed. I remember my brother crying and pleading with me not to leave. He had come to love my fiancé as they were buddies. My heart raced in fear and I knew this was irreparable. I went to his mother and asked if I could stay with her for a night or two until I figured things out. I was after all driving one of her vehicles, since I had lost mine. She supported me fully and even went with me the next day to pack what I could. Looking back, I believe she thought I would return or that I was exercising some form of tough love. It was hard. I did not miss a class and it was finals week. I went to work and school and stayed strong though I wanted to curl up in a ball and cry. I called home and gained some clarity in conversation with my mother. The next day, I returned with his mother by my side and knocked on the door. When he opened the door, his mother and I announced we were there to get my belongings. He let us in and his mother sat down by the front door. I began to nervously retrieve my belongings, all while my brother was in school. As I picked up my clothes and hurriedly put them into garbage bags, he began hovering around me. He threatened suicide if I left him. He sobbed as I grabbed what I could. I could hardly stand the guilt he was baiting me with to stay. As I looked around, I realized none of it mattered. I could not listen to him any longer. I packed one bag of my clothes, and as I sought my most prized belongings, I found he had destroyed them the evening prior. I was very hurt. I grabbed what little my brother had and walked to the car. I gave his mother a hug and asked if I could keep the car for a month until I found new transportation. She obliged. That night, my mother overnight-expressed my birthday card. It was my 21st birthday. I will never forget it. It was a smiley dancing bear with a glass of wine in its paw. My mother has always had a thing for bears. I smiled as I opened the card, and then I cried as a check for $1,000 fell out and she wrote, "Here is to the best and rest of your life!"

I put a down payment on an apartment, cut off all ties with his family, bought egg mattresses for my young brother and me, and two fern plants. I put food in the fridge and called it home. I felt safe. Once I felt safe, I called A Safe Place after being referred there by my Employee Assistance program through work. A Safe Place is a non-profit organization providing support for women in relationships with domestic violence. While I was not a victim of domestic violence in my mind, I began attending a support group. As I shared with other young women, I learned the red flags. It became clear I was in an unhealthy relationship. The warning signs are not usually that easy to see. People often can excuse or ignore red flags for many reasons.

[2]Here are some warning signs that your relationship may be abusive. Your partner:

1   Tries to control your behavior

2   Tells you who you can be friends with or isolates you

3   Wants to know where you are all the time

4   Calls or texts you excessively

5   Blames you for problems

6   Is obsessed with your relationship

7   Feels he or she owns you and has certain rights over you

8   Criticizes you frequently – your appearance, intelligence, ability to make decisions, etc.

9   Humiliates you in public

10  Makes you uncomfortable

11   Doesn't want to meet or be around your family or friends

12   Is extremely jealous of your friends and family

13   Accuses you of cheating

14   Angers easily

15   Makes it important to keep him/her from getting angry

16   Makes you afraid of what will happen if you end the relation-ship

17   Threatens you, makes you afraid

18   Has been abusive in past relationships

19   Says he/she can't live without you

20   Abuses siblings, friends, and/or animals

I had begun to accept the unhealthy pattern in my relation-ship. I had to be honest with myself to understand how I lived with – and almost married – a closet alcoholic. I'd been betrayed. I did six months of solid work for myself. Essentially, I added coun-seling sessions to my school courses and workload and focused on understanding how I had put myself in this position. I learned that I had some co-dependent tendencies. I've always had good intentions, but I haven't always had good boundaries. I was trying to take care of good people who were making poor decisions, and instead of holding those people accountable for their decisions, I was taking on a martyr's role. I realized that I was choosing rela-tionships where I needed to feel needed. This is unhealthy.

I did a great deal of emotional work to overcome the patterns of my behavior. Once I became clear, felt the pain – the raw emo-tion – and forgave myself, I made a choice to find the blessing in it all. There were many lessons in every choice and every outcome. I had created my reality, and now I was ready to repackage it and reclaim me!

It seemed like forever, but I finally graduated with an associates' degree and was planning to transfer to Roosevelt University. When my mother came to my graduation, we decided that it was time for my brother to return home with her. I had a new focus. I worked on trying to be 21 years old.

"B" – our belief – is what we do with what is put upon us. We must truly look at what our life mirrors to us so we can see the unconscious ways in which "A" – the adversity – has affected our outlook on life. If I had grown up witnessing healthy relationships, perhaps I would have recognized the red flags sooner. Many of the red flags in my relationship seemed normal to me at the time. I didn't even question them until my brother lived with us, and even then, I talked myself out of my innermost thoughts and rejections of what was healthy or normal. My intuition had provided warning signs early on, but I glossed over them for the sake of my desires. I saw my world as I wanted to see it, not as it was. Only when I chose to confront my reality did it become clear. In the end, I could only look at myself in the mirror. My fiancé and I came together as two people who were eager to have someone to love and be loved by. We dropped boundaries quickly, bypassing friendship and becoming a couple rapidly. Don't get me wrong – this can happen in healthy relationships too. But in my now-healthy relationship, I know I love my husband unconditionally, but I don't *need* him. I know he doesn't need *me*. We choose each other as equals and can be apart from each other (though we may not like it), feeling secure in our solid bond of love. We don't expect nor do we want to get all of our needs met through one another.

Coming out of the failed engagement, I had to take time to reflect on my behavior patterns in relationships. I was raised by a single mother. Through no intention of her own, she had to work and was gone a great deal when I was young. However, as I became a young woman, I had to address that growing up with an unreliable or unavailable parent means taking on the role of caretaker and/or enabler. My mother was always there for me, but not always physically present, so I had put myself into a parental role at a young age. A child in this situation puts the parent's needs first. As a result, I had learned to repress my own emotions and disregard my own needs so I could focus on the needs of my perceived "unavailable parent." When "parentified" children become adults, they *repeat the same dynamic in their adult relationships.*

While I was so busy taking on other people's problems, I failed to see my own issues and the fact that I was bypassing my own needs. I had allowed an imbalance to exist. With imbalance comes an imperfect energy center. Growing up with my healer mother, I knew I'd have to work on my energy center as well as my behavior patterns. When people are in a co-dependent relationship, one or both will have what psychologist Carl Rogers called a "satellite relationship." In my case, it was school and work. For others it could be drinking, obsession with a child, or an affair. Only when I removed myself from other people's problems could I see what it was about *me* that allowed it. What was *my* real need? I had become so busy with outward activity that I had practically all but silenced myself from my own intuition. Once I took the time to acknowledge my intuition and hear my own voice, I could see the wholeness of all the patterns, behaviors, and choices that I was enabling. I could understand how this came to be. I found clarity, and there is no way to work around the truth that our energy centers hold and attract. I repackaged all of it, and from that point forward, it was about me and my balance. Being desperate to help everyone else's pain had become too much for me to carry.

After working through it, I was able to open my heart and be ready for the next relationship with positivity rather than fear, with trust rather than distrust, and with radiance rather than bitterness. Self-love for the sake of love. Self-protection for the sake of self-transcendence. Self-transcendence for the sake of self-actualization, and self-worth for the sake of finding the happiness we all deserve. Our ability to assimilate our experiences and synthesize wisdom brings us to compassion and gratitude.

The result of focusing on my energy centers helped me to achieve a new state of balance. I began to experience life, find healthy solutions to problems, and enjoy a greater level of self-acceptance. We can often fool ourselves and others about how we feel about ourselves, life, pain, and relationships. But there is no way around the truth that our energy centers hold, and what that attracts is the mirror of what you carry in your soul.

We all deserve happiness. No matter what is put upon us in the form of "A," "B" is what we take from it. Our souls need the facts from every experience to grow and evolve. We must accept that energy is with us whether we acknowledge it or not. A lesson comes from every exchange and/or experience. We can choose to stay in the emotions of an experience or process the emotions and rise above the experience so we can derive the facts we need to move forward and evolve.

It was incredibly difficult to accept that I had been lied to and betrayed by someone I loved. It was also difficult to disrupt my home and walk away without a plan. Nonetheless, I did it. The hardest emotion to work through was the self-directed one. How did I miss this reality right before me? How did I live with a man who was drinking and never witnessed a single symptom of alcoholism? How did I accept an abusive relationship that I had adapted to? How did I become the guardian of my younger brother? How did I end up working two jobs to provide for us?

Now, I know how all that happened. It was to appease another human being and thus avoid conflict. I had defaulted to imbalance in order to sustain harmony. I removed myself from home for most hours of the week. That's never healthy if it means you're changing who you essentially are. Our truth is God's truth. When I left everything behind and started again from nothing, I knew it was my truth and the right thing the moment I sat with it. I felt free. Looking back, I needed to hit rock bottom to gain the knowledge to become a better version of myself. I moved forward only with the fact that this actually happened. I played a role in this reality, and only I could stop it from being my reality going forward.

How did I reclaim happiness? There are a few steps I worked through to honor and heal emotions. In the *Presence* tools for this principle, I will show you some exercises to reclaim happiness at its foundational level. To affirm to yourself that you're a child of God, you must first believe this to be true. At the soul level, you know what's right and what's wrong in its most basic principles among all humanity. In my faith, we are all born of original sin. Sin is our universal experience, but this is not what God intended for us – in the past or in the future. Each of us can choose to live in "Christ Consciousness." Some express their faith through religion, but you don't need to practice religion to feel close to God. I believe that any person can be saved from sin through Christ. Each of us can receive God's grace. To move through negative emotions and release negative energy, we must move through God's grace to reveal happiness. The Bible sets forth that human beings are intended to be "full of grace," and who we are is revealed and redeemed through God's saving power. To believe you are a child of God and be present in God's love, you must believe that even if you don't feel worthy of God's love, God's grace is upon you.

To deny this is to be without God, and I believe to be without God is to choose to be stuck. This is a dark state. I was stuck in the emotion of betrayal and sadness, guilt, and fear for months after my car was repossessed and I learned that my fiancé had lied to me. I tried to work through that with him, but as soon as I knew that effort was unequal between us, I chose to leave. To stay would have been to deny my truth, my "Christ Consciousness" to acknowledge what is right and just with my intuition and alignment with God. I chose God and left. Often, this can be very subjective, very heartfelt, and not diagnostic in nature.

You may not need a reason to move forward. In fact, I don't recommend waiting for some catastrophic event to occur if you already know your truth. Call it intuition. Your intuition is your knowing, your truth, despite all tangible reasoning. To trust your intuition takes faith. I would like to believe that you've heard your intuition whether you connect it to God or not.

Through this book, I hope to help you strengthen your openness to receive your personal power, your right to choose. I desire that you declare your strength to move forward and claim your true self. Are you ready to find the happiness you deserve? Ready to release the emotions that hold you back from true joy? Believe in your ability to activate your intuition to the possibility of living a rich and meaningful life. "B" is yours to choose ... every day, every moment, and every second. *You choose.* Reclaim your power to choose. Open your heart and mind to the ability to see things as they are, accept things as they are, and move into today with a clear conscience and presence.

## Energy

All living things carry a vibration. Your life force is a vibration. All things that once had life carry a vibration. For example, my mother can feel the love that is in a wood table. The table carries energy even though you or I may see it as a dead tree. It once lived, thus it has a vibration. For example, everyone has had a friend who has had a terrible day. You ask what is wrong and your friend begins to share the story with you. When you came in the room you felt good. Now you begin to feel down and you may notice your friend begins to feel better. You shared some of your life force vibration or your energy with them. Energy can be positive or negative. Energy must always balance to equal when positive energy and negative energy share the same space. This is how we leave pieces of ourselves behind. Your energy can be loaned to others all day every day and it can leave you depleted. Essentially, the higher vibration source leaves the room with a lower vibration and the lower vibration source can pull from the higher vibration source in the moment the energies are converging. It is part of God's perfect plan. The only thoughts in your head, the only feelings in your being, the only vibration in your body should be the ones that God gave you and God words and God's thoughts to you. Invocation prayers can help you stay sovereign with God. To do this, you must have presence in this moment.

PRESENCE TOOLS 2 - FIND THE HAPPINESS YOU DESERVE

───────── MENTAL REVERSAL ─────────

This is an exercise to replace something negative in your experience and use your personal power to recreate it to move to gratitude. To do this, you must take yourself through meditation to a mental place of focus. You can close your eyes and take yourself to a place of healing. For some, it is healing to be near water, for example. One might take a candlelit bubble bath and do this exercise. Another might go to a lake or shore and visualize the letting go of the images so that they can move through the emotion and file it away as fact without emotion. This can be done with almost anything and it can be exercised as a daily practice to move into the present moment each and every day.

Before you begin, consider the way in which you relate to the memory, the emotion and the facts of the situation. **If you are Visual** you can close your eyes and practically visualize anything in your mind as it is said to you. You may visualize events with pictures vs. words. You will be able to recall the memory event and see it with your eyes closed, just as it is when your eyes are open. This is a Visual way of recalling and it can be done with past or present traumas or injuries or even in future manifestations of desired outcomes.

**If you are Kinesthetic**, you feel your world primarily and learn either through personal experiences, personal examples, or by doing or practicing through some form of simulation. You can feel your world. For example, you could imagine rain drops hitting your face, the taste of a food you like or a drink that refreshes or comforts you. You can smell fresh-baked cookies and although there may not be any in the room at the time, you are able to sense them.

**If you are Auditory**, you learn in an auditory or aural way. You are able to hear a memory. Perhaps the sounds, what was said, and you can recall things you heard in the past. For example, you may recall your inner voice, a dog barking in the background, a siren blaring, even conversations of friends and gatherings. People who have this as their preferred learning style will report that they learn best from lectures, group discussion, radio, email, using mobile phones, speaking, web-chat and often by simply talking things through.

**If you are a Read/Write** learner, you prefer everything in words. You may have enjoyed essays, books, lists and reports. You may write things out fully before presenting them and you search for words behind the pictures. Actually, writing your memory out as it happened, and then rewriting it as you would have liked to have recalled it will help you work through the steps of Mental Reversal.

**Step One:** Think of the experience, the event, or the trauma from the beginning to end. Replay it to relive it in your mind. Louise Hay was a remarkable metaphysical healer and has been instrumental in helping many understand that thoughts create our life experiences, and that the key to true happiness is self-love. The first step in loving yourself is allowing everything you want to flow naturally. Her mantra in my mind, was "What you feel you can heal!" So, as you go to the beginning of what "A" was, you must breathe it, smell it, taste it, and even hear it in your mind's eye. It is imperative to live it again in your mind. Put yourself in the moment from the beginning. You must feel to heal. Play it like a movie in your mind. See it fully from beginning to end. If it was years of negativity and it is still happening, play it from first instance to current day.

**Step Two:** Feel! Be present in the feeling, the emotions. Honor the emotions.

**Step Three:** Take a cleansing breath. Now rewind the movie to the beginning when it started.

**Step Four:** From the beginning, recreate a whole new movie. Create it scene by scene in your mind. What should have happened? What would have been the preferred sequence of events? Visualize the "NO!" that should have stopped it, and how it would have felt and looked with Christ's love in it. For example, if your boss, your husband, your friend, you name it, is never nice to you, then have that person doing pleasant things in your mind's eye. If you were assaulted, just go back to the beginning and visualize them listening and stopping when you said, "NO!" Recreate the day or situation to the present moment. Mentally pull it from your survival mode/reaction to your frontal lobe or your consciousness in thought. The function of the frontal lobes of our brains involves the ability to project future consequences resulting from our current actions. It is the place where we make the choice between good and bad actions, or even better and best choices. This is our conscience. By recreating it visually as a scene in our mind, we play it out again in replay. It will be brought into your frontal consciousness as facts from the present perspective not with the emotion of the past.

## PRESENCE TOOLS 2 - FIND THE HAPPINESS YOU DESERVE
# ———— INVOCATION PRAYERS ————

These are special prayers that can be said daily. These are for-giveness tools. When properly used, they allow you to become mentally and spiritually present in every day. Whether your day is good, bad, ugly, or indifferent, you can release the negative energy through prayer. Essentially, we try to keep our own posi-tive energy, but we naturally give our positive energy to a negative person or anyone with a lower vibration than ourselves. Their force pulls it from us, and these prayers can restore you to your natural positive state, ultimately protecting your energy. By send-ing them positive energy in prayer, we get our energy back rather than leaving pieces of ourselves and our energy stores to others.

These prayers should be used in conjunction with Mental Reversal meditations, but you can pray them as often as you like. These are tools for life. These special prayers can take you from the sorrow, guilt, fear, and negative feelings, and move you through prayer and thought to release the negative energy vibration. You can transpose that energy and release it with compassion and gratitude for the lesson and for the mere fact that you survived (by the grace of God) to receive the lesson. This prayer can be good for prayer requests specific to those who have passed on, thus releasing us from some form of energy that holds us back due to missed opportunity or the feeling of missed communications. The prayers invoke blessings with the sovereignty of God. Your energy will come back to you as the same positive expression and wish you are sending to in prayer to the other person. Once you are in the present moment without the triggers from yesterday, you can be fully present in today. The difference between prayer requests and prayer demands is that prayer requests are made to God directly and intended as such. Prayer demands are your requests from God to be sent to another living person. Key differences in application and practice are noted below the headers for each prayer.

## Invocation Prayer Requests

(Perform immediately when something happens that affects your energy)

(Can be prayer for infant children)

(For those who have passed on/dead people or pets)

I, _____ **(your full name),** request that all psychic chords with _____ **(insert their name)** be severed and seared and sent to the Great Central Son to be transposed and sent back to them as **(blessings): (Insert all you intend and pray for in the form of blessings back to the person and keep in mind your blessings should include all that they may need). You must always begin the blessings with these four intentions and then you may add to them. Initial four intentions should be unconditional love, *joy*, compassion and sovereignty in addition to other blessings you may pray for to include: self-love, peace, forgiveness, wholeness of heart, communication, truth, spiritual growth, self-direction, self-discipline, self-actualization, etc.**

I request this as my birthright.
    I empower it with:
    God the Holy Father, God the Almighty
    Christ the Great Central Son
    And the Holy Supreme being within me.

I then release it forth to the Universe, to be balanced and harmonized to the good of God and all living things.

Because I request this, let it be done. (Amen)

## Invocation Prayer Demands

(Perform immediately when something happens that affects your energy) Examples: arguments, accidents, negative things in past or present

(Can be prayer for everything living)

(Daily Prayer)

I, _____ **(your full name),** demand that all psychic chords with _____ **(insert their name)** be severed and seared and sent to the Great Central Son to be transposed and sent back to them as **(blessings): (Insert all you intend and pray for in the form of blessings back to the person and keep in mind your blessings should include all that they may need). You must always begin the blessings with these four intentions and then you may add to them. Initial four intentions should be unconditional love,** *joy,* **compassion and sovereignty in addition to other blessings you may pray for to include: self-love, peace, forgiveness, wholeness of heart, communication, truth, spiritual growth, self-direction, self-discipline, self-actualization, etc.**

I demand this as my birthright.

I empower it with the full power of;

God the Holy Father, God the Almighty

Christ the Great Central Son

And the Holy Supreme Being within me

And with Archangel Michael

And with the High Priestess Quan Yin

I then release it forth to the Universe, to be balanced and harmonized to the good of God and all living things.

Because I demand this, let it be done *Now!* (Amen)

## Invocation Prayer Multi-Dimension/Multi-Faith

(Perform daily at the beginning of and end of each week.)

(Can be prayer for anything that holds energy)

I, _____ **(your full name),** request that all psychic chords with every one, every place, every plant, every animal, everything within this dimension and all other dimensions be severed and seared and sent to God Almighty, the High Priestess Quan Yin, and the Gods and Goddesses of all the dimensions within all the Universe and all the solar systems, to be transformed as *joy*, unconditional love, sovereignty, love, Compassion Bliss, Euphoria, Vibrancy, Vitality and the Highest Form and Beauty in which their dimensions allow.

I demand this as my birthright.

I empower it with the full power of:

God the Holy Father Almighty

The High Priestess Quan Yin

And all Gods and Goddesses of all the dimensions within all the universes and all the solar systems; and the Holy Supreme Being within me.

I demand them to be balanced, harmonized and unified to their Gods and Goddesses highest notification and frequency with their dimensions allow. To the good of God and all living things.

Because I demand this, let it be done now. (Amen)

# PRESENCE PRINCIPLE 3
## The Empowering Lens

*"Above all else, guard your heart,
for everything you do flows from it."*

–PROVERBS 4:23

## One Day At A Time

One day at a time I rebuilt my life. The fact that you are taking time to read this book tells me you are seeking joy, and you may even be seeking purpose. Just by reading, you can be manifesting something positive in your life. You will know what is right for you. Trust yourself and have faith that when the time is right, all will be revealed.

As you go about your day, it is important to open your senses to all that is good. I spoke on a panel in recent weeks to an audience of young girls seeking to be entrepreneurs. The Young Entrepreneurs Academy (YEA!) is a groundbreaking and exciting program that transforms local middle and high school students into real, confident entrepreneurs. Through the year-long program, students in grades 6-12 generate business ideas, conduct market research, write business plans, pitch to a panel of investors, and launch their very own companies. It was remarkable how the experience brought me to recall habits or characteristics that I had built upon. Questions revolved around our younger years. What did we do when we were their age? Such a humbling moment to have a room of 50 to 100 or so young girls and their parents seeking your wisdom. I was one of four female CEOs. I was truly inspired by these young girls. Reflecting on my own childhood, I certainly can tell you I never once thought I would be an entrepreneur. I found myself sharing that it was really important to take it one day at a time. I never said to myself that I was getting a bachelor's degree while working full-time. I simply went to work one day at a time and took each course with my sole focus on that semester. Never did I consider the daunting prospect of working and then going to school at night only to do it over and over again. I freed myself on Friday nights and certainly I enjoyed nights out with my girlfriends but I was diligent to keep focus on my responsibilities. I can even recall my girlfriends dancing in the early morning hours after the sun had risen and we had retired to our apartments. I would be pounding out homework for my 9:00am class Saturday morning. Why? Because I had outlined my plan. I had begun with the end in mind. I had inquired to those I looked up to. How did they get where they are? What did they study and learn? I had done enough in my chosen field at 21 to know that a degree was the ticket to play the game. It didn't necessarily matter what you learned but rather that I could prove that I can learn. Little did I know that the experience I was gaining by working would catapult my career.

In the early 1990s, businesses were downsizing and rightsizing and I had walked more people out of their jobs in my corporate experience than I had hired. Often, what we dream for ourselves is not the reality. Instead, people put all their hopes into a job, a promotion, sometimes even a person, only to see it all come crashing down. It is painful. We have all been there.

## Dreams Are Not Always What They Seem

The day had finally come. I will never forget how excited I was. I think I had dreamed I would work in the city (Chicago) ever since I had graduated high school and moved from Montana. I landed my first job in HR management at the age of 23. I felt as though I had finally made it. I no longer had to work two jobs. I only had one more year of school to complete my bachelor's degree. I was in a solid relationship with a man I loved, two years strong. I had met him shortly after my 21st birthday and he was the person who helped me believe in love after my first adult relationship of abuse and deceit. It seemed all was as I had desired it to be. And yet, within six months I was ill. Not just with the flu, or a cold or something that you get over. I had experienced a complete flare-up of a childhood condition I lived with but often denied. Sure, I lived with pain due to my childhood arthritis and, yes, I sought out a rheumatologist when I was 18 only to be diagnosed with fibromyalgia. I had always managed the pain around my busy life before, but this was different. I was unable to get out of bed. I had extreme fatigue, and felt like I could barely walk. Every muscle in my body hurt, and not like the soreness you feel after you work out but more like an all-over tenderness that makes daily life a struggle. I suddenly was not motivated, I was sad, and felt tremendous guilt for this wonderful company that had just hired me and placed me into a key role. I took a leave of absence.

Over a period of months, I grappled with the crazy reality that I was 22 and about to file for disability. I had no choice but to resign my position. I was devastated.

It took months for me to realize I was wearing rose-colored glasses once again. My heart had been telling me for some time that I wasn't happy. Yes, the job was great but I was commuting two hours in traffic to and from work each day. I missed trees and open spaces and, I don't know, the people who just say, "hello" as you walk past. I had changed my whole life for this job. I was covering 50-plus miles each day to get from work, to school, to home and there was little time left to think, let alone "be" with myself. My boyfriend at the time was caring and supportive of me during this challenging time. As I began to come to terms and accept what my heart truly wanted, I began to heal, and freed myself of all that was not in alignment with my heart's desire. No matter how one tries to avoid the root of a problem, hide the real pain, or in some cases even try to control the outcome, healing takes place when and where it is needed. Opening your mind to the blessing of the healing is the true gift.

It just so happened that my truth included leaving my boyfriend, someone I loved. It was hard, and painful. He had always been good to me but one conversation led to another and he had shared that he did not know if he wanted to have children (in the future). As he spoke those words, it was as if a dagger had cut right through my heart. Hearing this truth was as important as accepting it. I did not try to change his mind. I did not speak how much I had hoped to be a mother one day as if to plead with him. In an instant, I knew that his truth was not my own and our relationship changed. I read once that the resistance of unpleasant change is the root of suffering. To invest in a relationship that would not lead to a family of my own one day meant I would suffer if I stayed in it. In an instant, I knew it was done. The universe had let me know this was not my future. Not knowing what was next, I packed my things and moved out. That same day I found myself soul-searching with a dear friend. She looked at me without judgment and asked, "If you could do anything right now, what would it be?" It was as if she gave me permission and yet the decision had been mine all the while. I looked back to her and stated, "I would give up living on my own, move back home, be a student for once during the day in my final year of undergrad, and be happy being just a student!" She looked back and said, "Then do it. You don't have to move back home to Montana. Stay here! Move in with us, go to school during the day and be happy. It is okay. You have enough experience to go back to work. It will always be there. Try acting your age, for once! When I was your age I was a cocktail waitress!"

I did exactly that. I moved everything out of my home with my boyfriend at the time, and let him know he could not take back what he said. He had hoped to reconcile but for me, the relationship was over. I moved back in with my family, enrolled in day classes for the spring, and I recall it as one of the happiest times of my life. I was healthy, I was learning and I was enjoying being just a student. I think I had always dreamed of what it would be like to just go to school. How amazing it must have felt to just study and not have the pressures of putting a roof over your head. It was like a dream. I had one semester left and for my final year of undergrad, I was just a student. Oh, and a cocktail waitress! I did have a car payment to maintain, after all! The answer is truly within you. Taking the time to self-reflect and feel safe in the question allows us to really reconcile to the answer.

## Healing Takes Courage

It is often times like this when we are not asking for anything from God that God delivers. I had worked at a dance club for six weekends. It was the middle of July and I was enjoying being young, healthy and single. I had no interest in relationships, commitments or anything that would deter my current focus of just enjoying my final semester of school. In fact, I had no interest in dating. One young man took a liking to me while I was working and over a series of attempts, he made it quite clear he was interested in getting to know me. One thing that differentiated him from many others, was that he actually made me blush when he fawned over me. There was an intrigue and chemistry that was undeniable.

When you work in a dance club, you come home with piles of cards and gratuities. I was practically numb to the flattery but something about this one man was different. He had said the most peculiar things to me in our brief exchanges that evening. He had captured my attention. It was nearly impossible to ignore, in fact. Yet, I was not ready for anything, not even dinner. Someone close to me took notice of the fact that it had been five months since my last relationship and I was not open to dating. I had not opened my heart for another. In fact, I had mentally closed myself off from love. She sat me down and helped me to realize that I was no longer in a relationship and yet, I was acting like I was. I had not let go of my prior relationship despite leaving him. I know I had some work to do. I took the time to journal and meditate and I opened my conversation with God through prayer. I practiced my invocation prayers and sent prayers of healing and forgiveness. I then took the time to really consider all I had learned, all I had desired for my future and I prayed for it. I then began to conduct my own due diligence. I asked around about the man, after all, I did have his home address, business address, emails and phone numbers. It turned out one of the women who got her nails done at the same salon I attended worked for him. I found myself asking about him and all was favorable. I thought, if his employees have positive things to say, he must be allright. Three weeks had passed and he never came into the club again. I decided to email him. He emailed back, "Sunshine on my shoulders makes me happy!" My personal email at the time had "Sunshine" in the domain. He replied and yet again asked for my number. I emailed him my phone number and waited. And waited. I was perplexed. Here was a guy who truly wanted my number and I finally give it and he doesn't call! Impatiently, I had a girlfriend come with me and we drove past his house. I kid you not, the moment I drove past his house to see if he was home, he was calling me. I returned home to his message. Needless to say, I called him back. We had a seven-hour conversation. We had our actual first date a month later and shared our first kiss. I went home that night and journaled that I thought I just had dinner with the man of my dreams. He was traveling on business that week and he called from abroad the next day to simply say, "I just saw the sun rise and I didn't want another day to go by without telling you, I love you." I sat speechless with that. We began dating and it took the attack on our country on September 11, 2001, for me to realize and admit out loud that I loved him too. My first instinct was not wrong. He is the man of my dreams as he just so happens to be my husband now.

The roller coaster of emotions that many will tell you is the undeniable recognition of your soul to another's and yet, it is terrifying to lose control of your own heart let alone trust it entirely to another person. I have found love is truly a leap of faith. A brave step in acknowledging that to love another human being unconditionally is to risk being hurt beyond repair, and to know that you would risk all of it for the sake of love itself. It took something even greater than myself to overcome the fear. It took the horror of the 9/11 terrorist attack on our country for me to admit to him what I already knew. It resonates with me how fearful I was to trust again. To witness the loss of life that day in order to begin cherishing life … it was a sad reality. I knew then, I had nothing to lose. I rushed to find him and share my truth immediately following news of the terror attack. I remember counting the minutes until he got off work. He truly was the first person I thought of after reeling from the shock of it all. To overcome my fear and embrace love was amazing. It was love like I had never known before. I can honestly say that my heart has been fully open ever since.

Becoming fully aware of my feelings in the midst of change is what allowed me to ride the wave of change. Detaching from my fear allowed me to gain acknowledgement of the present and move into the future. Taking this step was a conscious choice to let go of the past, embrace the blessings before me and trust the future. I moved from one space to another by working through acceptance, forgiveness and faith.

To trust oneself fully is the basis of the truth found only in your intuition. It can be scary or it can be beautifully exciting. Each of us is empowered with the ability to embrace conscious change. I encourage you to embrace the greatest mystery of soul growth! That being, how your soul knows at any given moment what is needed for realization, self-awareness and growth.

In the years that led up to this shift in my life, I had worked to clear old dysfunctional patterns that had kept me from feeling full joy. I truly believe every change I moved through has led me to the experiences whereby I have gained insight. All has led me to this very moment now with you. Mental clarity and spiritual enlightenment require a desire to move through change rather than to stagnate in it. Depending on your comfort level, a therapist or healer can act as a clear mirror to your inner reality. In an unbiased environment, you can have a trusted confidant who will reflect back your attitudes, ideas, and emotions, so that you can see yourself and your choices with greater clarity. Personally, I find the practice of journaling very helpful for identifying patterns of behavior. I have journaled consistently throughout my life. The mind is a wonderful thing and it is amazing how day in and day out we can forget what happened last week, last month, even if it was pivotally important. Through journaling, I have found it easier to hold myself accountable to not only what I desired but what I would not tolerate. Often, speaking your reality to a most trusted confidant is the beginning of healing. You surely have a friend who can help you stay accountable to yourself. Be brave and open up to them. If they love you, they will be there without a doubt!

## Energy Is All Around You

For centuries, the ancient wisdom-keepers and healers in several traditions had a keen understanding of the energetic body. The healing traditions from China, India, Japan and Tibet, as well as other countries, all have spoken of energy channels, meridians or Nadis along which the vital energy flowed. You can spend a lifetime learning about all that is energy and one can meet many healers throughout the world. Given the global context and faith origins, I came across a rather straight forward explanation that I have come to like. The concept of Chakras is found particularly in the tantric traditions of Buddhism, Hinduism and Jainism. They are conceived as an energy focal point, bodily functions or psychic node in the subtle body. Subtle bodies make up our human energy system. The Chakra theories are elaborate part of the Kundalini system. These theories differ between the Indian religions, with esoteric Buddhist literature mentioning four Chakras, while eso-teric Hindu texts are stating seven. They are believed to be part of the subtle body, not the physical body, and connected by energy channels called Nadi. In the Kundalini version of yoga, breath exercises focus, in part, on mastering and channeling energy through Chakras.

The word Chakra is an Indian expression that derives from the Sanskrit word meaning "wheel," as well as "circle" and "cycle." One of the Hindu scriptures Rigveda mentions Chakra with the meaning of "wheel," with ara (spokes). According to Frits Staal, Chakra has Indo-European roots, and is "related to Kuklos (Greek) from which comes English cycle, Latin circus, Anglo-Saxon hveohl and the English wheel. "However, the Vedic period texts use the same word as a simile in other contexts, such as the "wheel of time" or "wheel of dharma," such as in Rigveda hymn verse. 1.164.11[3].

Traditional Chinese medicine originated in ancient China and has evolved over thousands of years. The Chinese say we carry ancestral energy in our kidneys. This is strongly related to the Root Chakra where the fight or flight syndrome is linked to the adrenal cortex of the kidneys. When we are stressed, adrenaline is pumped into our blood, giving us the energy to stand our ground or flee from danger. The kidneys can give extra reserve to get something done, ultimately to survive. The Chinese refer to this as the Seas of Reserve and it has been widely studied and referred to as the source of their medical model of energy medicine around this concept.[4] We all can benefit by knowing how to conserve our energy to restore vitality. Giving our energy away to people who do not fortify us quite simply depletes our Spirit. And the same happens when we give energy to something that does not support us. Most disease can be attributed to a basic overtaxing of energy. Changes can show us blockages in our energy, the dark spaces where healing is needed to return to a fuller, more radiant life.

Growing up with my mother as a healer has given me an awareness of how energy moves through me and how my energy can affect others. I have also learned how negative energy can be present, how it can make me ill, and how it can be freed. Throughout my life, my mother always referred to this as "energy" or my "life force." I regard energy as important, and while I respect what I do not know about the ancient knowledge of Chakras, I do know that what I feel is real, and that what I feel, I can heal.

## PRESENCE TOOLS 3 - THE EMPOWERING LENS
# — RECOGNIZING YOUR ENERGY BLOCKS —

*May this guide take you through this exercise with greater presence and application to work through deeper energy blocks you may come to recognize.*

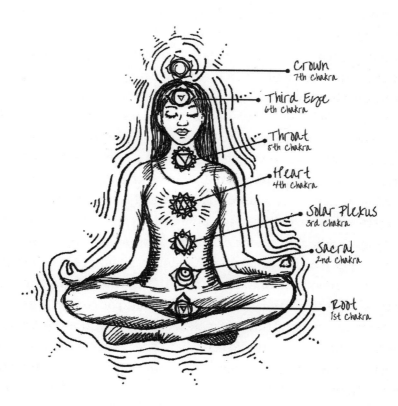

## **Your Lens**

The empowering lens will require you to know what type of learner you are. This is recommended as you begin to discover your empowering lens. The reason your learning style becomes relevant is because in order to use your empowering lens to open your energy blocks, you must know how you process information. However you learn is how you stored your experience, your feelings, and your information. To truly bring it forth, you need to recall your memory in such a way that it brings you to write it out, draw a picture or conceptualize your experience in such a way that you can go back and apply the tools in Chapter 1 and Chapter 2. As you work through your thoughts, put them down on a piece of paper. Truly expel the negative memory from you by writing it out, drawing the picture, truly feeling it again, or listing it line by line. As you do this, aim to feel it in the learning style that is dominant to you. As you learned or experienced this memory, you must unlearn the experience in the same way. Now you are ready to *Mentally Reverse* it and state your *Invocation Prayer.* If you have your piece of paper before you, once you are done you can go so far as to burn the piece of paper and dispel it from you forever. Watch your negative memory and emotions drift in the breeze and feel free and clear of them.

As you gain this empowering lens, ask yourself if you are living in the past. The past keeps you from moving forward. Look honestly and deeply into yourself. Remove every distraction and focus on your truth. You do need silence and quiet time to reflect on your connections to energy or your lack thereof. Seek a space where you can breathe ... breathe in, center yourself and breathe out. Keep an open mind, open heart and be kind to yourself in thought and affirmation. Remember to feel. You must feel, even if it is painful, you must feel it to heal it. Some can benefit from guided imagery or guided meditations. If this is difficult to do on your own, seek support. There is a tremendous amount of resource with respect to this subject. **Begin by looking within your own mind and heart:**

1    Ask yourself, am I feeling my world?

2    How am I feeling my world?

**3**  Or, do I just exist because it is safe or so horrible because I am beaten down and feel lifeless?

**4**  Are you aware of the wrong things around you?

**5**  How do you feel your life force shutting down?

**6**  How is joy blocked through your current relationships?

Common symptoms or energy blocks can act as indicators of your imbalance with energy. Remember, when you have blocked energy you can become numb to anything that comes in or through you.

You can have an energy block in any Chakra and ultimately it can diminish your life force. Each Chakra is linked to another through the flow of energy and ideally you want clear flows of energy running through each of your Chakras, adding to your vitality and radiance. A Chakra is never fully blocked but your choices, behaviors and subsequent ailments, emotions and outcomes are all tied to your energy centers. The entire framework for your energy is based on who you are as a human being. Often, we can be in relationships or making decisions without a second thought as to what it does to affect our energy or the energy of others.

There is accountability behind every choice. Let's talk examples.

I met a woman many years ago who was committed to a married man. Relationships like this are simply wrong to many of us. However, she was in love with this man and despite all the disappointments and truths that he was promised to another, the relationship carried on for nine years. One question directed at her was this, "If he left her and promised himself to you in action, would you still want him?" Amazingly, that resonated with her and she ended the relationship. She freed herself for what she truly desired. When you are with the wrong person for the wrong reason, like sex addicts, there is no heart in it whatsoever. Dating a married person or engaging in an affair with someone can put hooks on your energy. These are symptoms that rob your life force from you, which lowers your vibration, and weakens you to a dependence on them for energy, which keeps you in the darkness and away from Christ- Consciousness. If you keep going back to a relationship that you know is wrong for you, it is a symptom that you have become numb. The other person's energy has weakened your energy and it affects you physically, mentally and emotionally. The positive manifestation of energy in relationships has the capacity to bring bliss, happiness, and harmony with another in unity and oneness.

Think of your body as a temple. To allow anyone into your vortex to share pleasure is to provide another access to one of your most powerful energy centers. Have you ever seen a woman or man who was physically attracted to another but it had no heart? Was it just lust or desire? I estimate you can answer, "yes" to that question. Perhaps it was you. If so, how did it make you feel? Is this person a higher energy or lower energy? Or is this person a spiritual equal? It may give you energy but is it sovereign with your heart? God's sovereignty means that there is not anything that will enter your life that God does not either decree or allow. For your heart to be sovereign with God would mean you believe that to be true.

Let's explore behaviors that emit blockages in your energy centers:

In your Root Chakra, your physical sense of safety and security affects your earthly energy. This Chakra is a source of well-being and it is foundational in nature. Blockages in this Chakra are typically revealed with ambivalence about the value of life.

In your Sacral Chakra, your relationships, including those of your lovers or your parents, can block your energy. Consider your view with pleasure and relationships. Perhaps you are detached from the intimacy in relationships. Was this learned, was it something you saw or is it something you desire because you are afraid of emotional intimacy? A blockage at this level can be physical. A true sign of balance is knowing who, what, and when is enough.

In your Solar Plexus, your soul lives. At our core is our esteem, our self-worth, and our confidence. Do you believe you are in control of your life? Do you love yourself? Do you feel you are enough? At some point in your life, you stop repeating old habits and learn from them. The emotions that are derived from blockages that may reside here can include anger, resentment, or even jealousy. If you feel you are a victim of circumstance, you may need to reconnect to your personal power. We all must do the work to prove our self-worth. The more you know who you are, the more brilliance you source from your Solar Plexus. Direct your life; do not fear that your feelings will be destructive if you let them out.

In your Heart Chakra, unhappiness, cynicism, and overall negativity are all signs of a clear blockage of energy. Suppressing our feelings can also lead to depression and sadness. All happiness comes from the heart. Trusting in love and joy, believing God opens doors. Self-destructive habits can keep you from hearing your Christ-Consciousness. This can be abuses of drugs, alcohol, food and an overall lack of self-accountability. Masking pain, suppressing pain, or blaming others for pain can block happiness. Obsessing with career or school or anything can bring an imbalance between work and play. How we look at life truly is reflected in our Heart Chakra. To truly love you must live without judgement or fear. To live with a trust that life is good opens the energy in the Heart chakra. Evaluate things in your life to whether it is helping you or hurting you.

In your Throat Chakra, a blockage can result when you are not facing something. Panic attacks, acid reflux, even poor sleep can result from not speaking your truth. You must speak your truth and even it if feels you must pull it out with rope, it is imperative to expel "it" out of you. Your voice matters, your truth matters, and fear of rejection is not worth the sacrifice of your energy.

In your Third Eye Chakra, you can be an intelligent and bright being – unless it's blocked. Then, you may lack wisdom. You may feel unappreciated or exhausted. Each cycle will feel different going in, but worse coming out. Repeated cycles or patterns indicate that you are not seeing clearly. A person can be visionary and look forward, but by putting blinders on, they may miss the beautiful blessings right before them. I once read a book called *Wisdom Bowls*[5] that included visualization exercises in which you "mended" your bowl. This made me realize that I was unable to even *visualize* every one of my bowls. The bowls were Wisdom, Vision, Joy, Love, Power, Intimacy, and Abundance. I learned that the cracks in our Wisdom Bowls taught us courage and grace as much as suffering and betrayal. By finding the meaning in my negative experiences, I was able to discover the way I was authentic and free from the past.

When your Crown Chakra is blocked, your spirituality is blocked. You may not hear God; you may be blinded by religion or what you have been taught. This can stem from put-upon information or a lack of information. This prevents you from not looking forward. Those who are aligned with their Crown Chakra have a clear and open channel to God. It is the source of all spiritual energy.

Treating symptoms will not recognize the problem. Life is a challenging journey. But recognizing the symptoms of blockages is critical to moving into the present moment with presence by overcoming the source of the problem, be it your way of thinking, the emotion you need to overcome or by seeing your every experience as a gateway to compassion and understanding. The tools, including the Invocation Prayers and Mental Reversals, come into play here. Recognizing energy blockages is the important part to getting to the real thoughts and emotions that keep us in the past. With this increased, empowering lens, I remain hopeful that you are not living with blinders on. Instead, I am hopeful you are spending time with yourself reviewing what is good for you, and is helping you know through your intellect but true to your heart-making decisions based on joy of the heart versus the loneliness of the heart. I have learned to work through lessons quicker and express gratitude more quickly, but I promise you it is a daily practice and the sooner you can get to a clean canvas, the sooner you can build on your joy and purpose. Healing can mean many things but to me it means adapting and moving forward with a better sense of balance than yesterday. What I do with my life today is what matters!

To arrive at "C" is to love each day to the fullest. Expect the unexpected, living in sovereignty with God and God's truths. You must believe in God to become sovereign to the fact that we do not have complete control over all that happens. Allowing yourself to not react but to respond without the triggers of the past, you are now able to move into tomorrow free and clear.

# PRESENCE PRINCIPLE 4

## *Capturing Dignity*

*"Do not be conformed to this world, but be transformed by the renewal of your mind, that by testing you may discern what is the will of God, what is good and acceptable and perfect."*

−ROMANS 12:2

### Unconditional Love

To this day, I can remember my first argument with the love of my life. When we first moved in together, I wanted to bring plants and other things into the space he once called his own. As I flitted about putting a candle here, a picture there, I thought some greenery would be ideal on our expansive living room wall mantel. Without hesitation, I added it to the décor. It was not long before I found that he had removed it! He worried that water would seep into the wood and warp it over time.

I was perplexed. That was not something I had thought of at all. To be honest, I could hardly believe we were having a disagreement over a *plant*. Needless to say, we came to a compromise after much drama. I considered his tastes, and I purchased a nice brass planter for the mantel.

In the months that followed, I learned just how meticulous he was. In the beginning, I would contribute to our household cleaning, but I quickly found that he would redo whatever I had done. Initially, it really hurt my feelings. At first, I took his gestures as generous and chivalrous. Once I learned what motivated him and what he truly needed, it was less enchanting. He needed to feel calm in his sanctuary, and I would be upset by his every move.

If not for my independent spirit, I could have easily manifested feelings of failure and low esteem. Instead, I learned to embrace that this was more about him and not me. Over time, it made sense. I took the time to look at life from his perspective. The fact that he had been in a family business with siblings and extended family for his entire had left him in a constant state of compromise. His home had become the one place where he could exercise his choice and sentiment.

In talking with my women friends, I usually found that the common complaints about their relationships were almost always about subjects that my love did perfectly – laundry, cooking, making the bed, contributing to the household duties, yard work. When I had friends over, I could enjoy an evening and let the "mess" wait until tomorrow. I learned that my love could not enjoy friends until the "mess" was in order. He cleans even when friends are over. During holiday gatherings, he never sits down with us. I have to remind him that it can wait. People are more important. Regardless, I have learned to appreciate his needs and at the end of the day, I accept him and just explain to my guests. Perhaps it was the boarding school he attended in his teenage years. He truly cannot relax when his bed is not made and everything is in order.

I believe that we're all made in the likeness of God. We all possess a certain grace from God. In the journey to live in harmony with an opposite that I loved, I had to seek to understand his motivations, his needs, his esteem-building activities, and his language of love. I'm now able to appreciate him, and I've learned when to help him let go. Early in our relationship, I expected romantic gestures. I would look for signs of thoughtfulness in gifts of flowers or cards. They never came. When I let him know I felt hurt by this, his reply amazed me. He believed that the fact that I have a nice, clean home with a manicured lawn meant I could feel proud to live in something he strives to provide. He shared the many other ways in which he is, in fact, thoughtful. He gave me a long list of gestures that I had never known about, let alone regarded. I realized that his language of love lasted 365 days a year, and it was not a series of Hallmark events.

Let me be clear. This man really should be working in forensics and solving crimes. He can tell when anything has been moved, when someone has been in our home, and if I leave something sitting out – even intentionally – it will be put back in its place promptly. He solves mystery messes from one end of our house to the other. I live in a pristine home, and our youngest son already cleans up after himself – at 22 months old!

I remember a dear friend counseling me before my marriage. She said, "Take the worst behavior about your love that bothers you and magnify it by 10! Can you live with that?" My answer was "Absolutely!" Everyone has pet peeves and idiosyncrasies. To each his own. However, I feel that God brought my love to me and, given this fact alone, I learn from him daily and he learns from me. We are ever-evolving and deepening our relationship with each other and with God. If someone's quirks don't bother you and they can accept yours, well then, count your blessings! The goal is to pair up with the one who will not drive you crazy and love them for all they are ... *as* they are.

## Blessings In Disguise

A year after we married, I had been working at a director level thirtyplus miles from home. At the time, I had also elected to work towards my graduate degree in the evenings. It was all-consuming! I look back and feel gratitude for my love. It is amazing he was still by my side after two grueling years. He was so supportive and empowering of my desires. I had wanted to start a family after we were married. After all, I was 28 when we married. I will never forget how he slowed me down and stated so simply, as he always does, "There is plenty of time for that! Finish your graduate degree and then we can worry about that! I know you will regret it if you don't go on to do it." He was right! I still thank him today for his practical sentiments. Two years flew by. I was two weeks out from commencement and final capstone presentations.

It was December 6, 2006, a Wednesday morning. It was freezing outside; the ground was wet and snow was on the sides of roads. Roads were icy but not intimidating to drive on. I am from Montana, after all! They do not even plow the roads in Montana. I packed up all I needed for the day, and rushed out the door in hopes to get to the office on time. I was so busy juggling my workload that I could feel the anxiety building in my chest. The overwhelming thoughts of how would I survive the next two weeks! I had all my work completed and it was time to execute, but I was exhausted. I relieved my anxiety by thinking of the end in sight. I was planning a celebration trip to Cabo San Lucas, Mexico, with my mother and a few favorite women in my life. I prayed daily, literally moment to moment to source my strength and breathe sanity.

Before I made it to work that morning, I was cruising about 45 MPH on a four-lane road known as Route 120 in northern Illinois. As I approached a busy intersection, I began to slow down to turn left. Within seconds, a truck was horizontal before me, maybe 10 feet away and I slammed on the breaks. As the front end of my car came in, the airbag deployed. I tasted blood in my mouth and I was knocked out for moment. Time stood still. I thought to myself, "I am alive," and then as if to say to God, I thought, "I wanted to slow down but you didn't have to do that!" Then came a rush of gratitude. I was alive. When I came to, I heard nothing, I saw what seemed like smoke inside my car so I frantically tried to unbuckle my seat belt. I exited the car and then I began to feel the pain. I was standing in oncoming traffic and the rest is a blur. I was placed on a spinal board and taken to a local hospital. In and out of scans and x-rays for hours. My mother showed up first as she was closer in proximity, but I wanted to see my love. Where was he? I would learn later, that someone in traffic grabbed my cell phone. In the days before password protection, this person was able to dial the first name in my contacts. The call went to Andrew. He was actually a coworker, someone who I worked a great deal with. In fact, I had likely spent more time talking with him then my husband. Many of us worked long hours. My love didn't carry a cell phone back then; in fact, he didn't carry a cell phone until 2009! Andrew had the painstaking task of trying to remember where my husband worked and then call through his business to find him. I was the Director of Human Resources, but ironically no one had my husband's work information. Thankfully he found him and I realized how this news shook him, when he eventually showed up at my side with his mother, who drove him. I suffered a grade 3 concussion, a broken nose, a sprained abdomen, a sacral torsion, disc herniation of L3 and bulging discs from L1 through L5.

I would live. I suffered. I hurt. I missed my capstone presentations. The girls went to Cabo San Lucas without me. In fact, the day they flew out, I was on a table with a therapist pushing my sacrum back in place. I felt very sorry for myself at the time. I could not feel the gratitude nor the compassion then. In the end, my schoolwork had been high enough, and I was granted my graduate degree without makeup but sacrificed a 4.0 GPA. I had to completely leave work, which was all I knew at the time. I was in my home, in my bed, being waited on by my love and I was miserable. I just wanted to go, go, go! God was teaching me something I knew nothing about at the time. I was learning how to just be. I was seeing my love before me for the first time in what felt like years. I was feeling the realities of where all my focus has been and where it needed to shift, especially if I were to be a mother. My husband's patience and keen sense of responsibility allowed me the time to heal. In retrospect, it was the gift of "shift." I never would be the mother I am today had I not had that trauma in my life! Had I not been slowed down to the point that I had no choice but to appreciate being slowed down. It took me a full year to heal both physically and emotionally. Then another year to recalibrate my life, embrace my permanent damage and move on after settling the legal dispute. And just when I thought it may never happen, we were blessed to move from "us" to "we" and we welcomed our first child.

## We Do Not Have To Be Stereotypes

To be blessed with a child is to feel as if God has come into the room with you. I feel truly blessed to be a mother and, interestingly enough, I had to learn what kind of mother I would be. It is everything and nothing that I expected. I had many preconceived and stereotypical notions. Now, as a mother, I thought I should tend to our home, take care of meals, provide a warm welcome-home greeting to my husband, and that my work would naturally be secondary. I resigned when I was pregnant so I could begin volunteering. My boss knew me well. He said, "Nicole, you're a workaholic! If you want to dabble in your work, dabble *here*. What do you want to do?" I said I wanted to be there just one day a week. He granted my request, and I partnered with him through the recession to downsize, and work through the challenges that were placing hard economic times facing man-ufacturers everywhere.

As I began to immerse myself in my role as a mother, I found true joy and happiness the entire first year at home. However, by the time my child was 15 months old, I became bored. What was so remarkable is that I was living put-upon expectations that weren't my own or even those of my husband. Perhaps my hormones set-tled, or perhaps I am just a busybody, but I really felt bored. I tried to suppress this feeling by planning special play times with my son around his naps. I took a board role in a mothers' group. I busied myself with play dates, trips to farmers' markets, and did "Lunch in the Park" on Fridays. My days were full, but my husband was working long hours, and I began to feel lonely. I tried to fully embrace my "mostly at home" role, but I also knew my son bene-fitted from independent play and quiet time for himself. I simply needed more engagement outside my home.

I had this incredible life, a loving husband, and a beautiful child, but the feelings of boredom quickly became feelings of guilt. I asked myself often if I would look in my son's eyes one day and say, "I chose to work even though I did not have to. I chose work instead of being home with you!" I did not feel the same joy as recalled feeling from my work, but I knew I could not commit to full-time joy. I began researching options for part-time engage-ments and quickly learned that, at my skill level, these were not easy to find.

Around this same time, I took part in my first silent retreat. If you knew me well, you would laugh at the possibility of me sitting quietly for something like this. I surprised myself, but it was only for one day. The retreat was full of faith-filled reflections, and one question was posed that changed my life – *What was the difference between fate and free will?* Of course, we all can write off various occurrences to fate or destiny. Some believe that fate is in our DNA. Others who are more spiritually guided will say that each of us is put on earth as part of a collective karma, as if we're destined to accomplish something in this life in accordance with our maker. Free will, on the other hand, is what we choose to do in any given moment. It's the "C" – the consequence.

I could have chosen to continue feeling less than radiant, but it is not my nature to stay thinking for long, only to dismiss those thoughts. Once I could delineate how I was feeling, I resolved that my current reality was not my destiny. Some people have the grace from God to be completely selfless and generous. I regard some as saints. I simply had more energy than my home could sustain on its own.

I asked myself, "Who am I?" I stripped myself of all of my roles. I did not want to believe that my job was in fact my *identity*. I needed to get deeper than that. I made a list and took away all the roles that came to mind: mother, daughter, sister, wife, director, friend, board member, woman, etc. I realized that those things were "me," but beyond the roles, *who am I?* What must I do through these roles to be me – to feel joy, to feel like I was living my God-given grace in service? I was so grateful and felt indebted to God.

I needed to find a way to use my graces to the benefit of others in service. I prayed for mental clarity and spiritual enlightenment. I began to write the results of the feelings those roles gave me. After the full-day retreat, I had left with three expressions that were at the core of *me*, the core of what I must do each day to feel happy despite my roles. If I could fulfill these three things, it would not matter whether I was at work or at home with my son. I knew that God had graced me with certain gifts that I personally must put to good work. There is a verse in the Bible that gave me perspective on this. James 2:18 reads, [6] "Indeed, someone might say, 'You have faith and I have works.'" Some interpret this as asking us to show our faith apart from our work, but then the reading challenges us to think with a clear and present awareness of the possibility that we could show our faith *by* our work. Before, I was blessed with feelings as a mother, but then the full awareness that, while being a mother changed me forever, it does not change who I am. I am a child of God who requires deep human exchanges through daily conversation. I am a child of God who requires making daily connections *with* people, *for* people, and *between* people. Just as I cannot rely on my husband to fulfill all of my happiness, I could not rely on my child to do so either. I was committed to being resourceful, generous, and kind in providing information, connection, and openness in the name of God for the benefit of others. I knew that without these three things – Connection, Conversation, and a Giving Exchange with people–I was not fully living. These were the three expressions I had come to realize were critical to living my gifts. Once I realized that while my role as a mother is my greatest work, I cannot be a good mother if I am not living my God-given radiance fully. When I knew this difference, I saw that I did not need to change who I was to be a good mother. And I finally had done the deep reflections necessary to come to terms with my truth and share it with my husband.

When I told my husband what I had decided, I requested his support so I could enter a two-year program for the lay ministry. I wanted to live in service, and he has afforded me the life to be able to do that. He heard me. And in his beautiful way, he replied,

"You love your work. Working with people in a business setting is what you do best, and I see it brings you joy. If the business world does not need some ministry, then I do not know what does!"

And just like that, my consulting practice was born. I asked my boss what he thought and, in response, I converted myself into a 1099 employee and he referred me to my first big client! I can honestly tell you that every exchange I have in my work, facilitated by my God-given graces, is in service to our Maker. So many people don't feel joy and purpose through their work. I believe in workplace ministry, and while it may seem covert, I would argue that I am rather *overt* about it. I pray that my children will feel the same joy and passion for their work, and that they may they find their fuel in their faith.

We have come so far since this pivotal moment back in 2010. My love has since retired, and people often ask me what he does all day. Ironically, he is busier now than when he worked. We both have positioned our gifts to work for our family, our faith, and our beautiful children – essentially, we are living a simple life based on simple truths. Opposites attract, but they surely have the ability to complement as well. Once we accepted who we each were and stopped trying to live up to stereotypes and preconceived notions, we learned that who we were as a couple is who we are as parents. My love would have never guessed that he would be the primary caregiver at home, and I never thought I would leave the corporate world to put out my own shingle. Ultimately, I have created my own playground at work. I structured my week to include time with my children, time with my husband, field time with clients, and work-from-home days to work *on* my business versus *in* it. I even carve out time to challenge myself physically. I have paid a trainer to make me go. Knowing what you will do and what you will not do is critical to building reinforcements in. I feel radiant and open to what must flex, as surely it will.

Life is full of surprises, and retaining our dignity through all the turns is of utmost importance. In our work, we all exercise choices each day. Often, daily conduct and our choices take us away from gratitude and service. We can become so busy and disconnected from the present that we pass people without saying, "Hello!" Even if we do not have money to give a homeless person, when we say, "God bless" or "How can I help you?" it raises our own personal dignity. The balance remains in our personal energy sources. It's important to take time to ensure that we avoid becoming stuck in our ego. Ego can have us weighing decisions with full choice as if no consequence exists, and the "I" becomes more important than the "we" in everything. In contrast and on the opposite end of the energy force field is "Woe is me!" and "What choice do I have?" These leave us to fate, chance, or destiny. The danger occurs when we reach a point where we are no longer at the helm of our own life experiences. The key to this principle is walking into the power of being true to yourself. This is optimized when you are in love with someone who truly loves you for being true to yourself and vice versa. With all your perceived ugly, less-than-perfect ways, God made you perfect just the way you are! The question is – do you believe it?

You might be surprised to know that my husband has yet to read my first published book, let alone this one. I love that he loves me with no makeup, bedhead, and without my works! It is the best feeling to have love that appreciates the simplicity of "you," role-free and with no expectations, just presence. In fact, my favorite sentiment from him is when he says I am beautiful from the inside out. I feel blessed to be in love, and I will always enjoy *wanting* him by my side vs. *needing* him by my side. We believe we are destined to evolve and grow in this life together. Best of all, he loves me beyond my roles, and my joy and purpose come from something much deeper than those many roles.

PRESENCE TOOLS 4 - CAPTURING DIGNITY

## CLARITY OF BEING

*May this guide take you through a reflective exercise to see your God-given gifts and bring you to a higher presence in daily living joy and purpose in service, service to the greater good as a child of God.*

## Journal, Breathe, and Ask Yourself:

What plans have you put off but still dream of?

_____

_____

What can you begin doing *now* to achieve your dream in the future?

_____

_____

Remove all titles, roles, relationships and ask yourself, "Who am I?"

_____

_____

What brings you *joy*? When do you lose time doing something?

_____

_____

Does that something bring you *joy*?

_____

_____

How does your life support the natural *joy* from within?

_____

_____

What God-given gifts do you possess?

_____

_____

How can you enhance your life by building your day to support yourself and *joy* through your God-given gifts?

_____

_____

List the ways you express and live Unconditional Love in your life.

_____

_____

List the ways others express and live Unconditional love towards you.

_____

_____

What blessings can be derived from these questions?

_____

_____

How can you grow to a greater capacity in love?

_____

_____

Do you have Clarity of Being?

_____

_____

Can you "just be" and be joyful?

_____

_____

# PRESENCE PRINCIPLE 5

## Becoming Authentic

*"Only the truth of who you are, if realized, will set you free."*

−ECKHART TOLLE

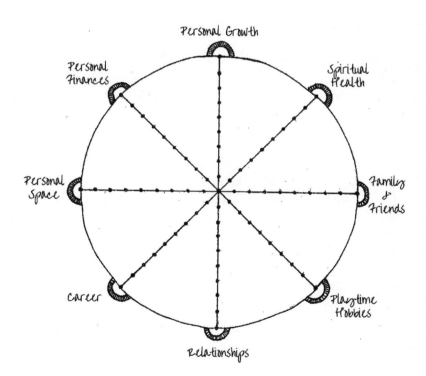

## Empowered By Love

Looking back, it is easy to see how empowering love can be. In my early twenties, I can admittedly say I was a people-pleaser. In high school, I was a good student. By my senior year, I was student body president, editor of the school paper and I managed to keep a job all throughout high school. Ironically, I never aimed for college and yet I found my way there. Having worked full-time and gone to school full-time, I was driven to succeed. Yet, success for me was always directed toward my independence. Once I had proven I could be self-sufficient, the definition of success changed.

Early in my relationship with my husband, my sense of security changed. I felt completely supported and safe, likely for the first time. This affected my level of truth in communications and assertiveness. I recall a time when I was a director, the sole female on a ten-person leadership team. I found myself speaking more directly than before. It was as if, suddenly, the truth mattered more than keeping my job. Ironically, it had a profound impact on my effectiveness in business. I clearly was not a "yes" person and working directly under CEOs, I learned the less "yes" people at the table, the better the outcome. It took me by surprise to find I was accepted by my peer directors and we had all realized good collaborative relationships. For nearly six years, I enjoyed my work thoroughly and it was not until I had my first-born child, and had partnered with my CEO to dismantle his business through the recession of 2008-2009, that I found myself bored. Perhaps my hormones had balanced, as my son was 15 months at the time. I knew I did not want a full-time demanding role in a new company. Yet, I had lived a wonderful experience of building an HR department from scratch for the third time and yet, this time, it was recognized as best in class. I wanted to feel that magic again. I elected to go on a mission, to begin consulting in search of another company that wanted to be a Best and Brightest® company to work for.

Having done the personal work to justify to myself why I desired to work, I began dabbling in consultative engagements. I had managed to positively frame that my desire to work was in fact my ministry. Within weeks of making this decision, two things happened. First, my CEO became my first client and he referred me to what would become my first Managed Service client on retainer. Second, a successful businesswoman who had known me for six years had asked me to speak at an event. In the weeks that approached, she learned that I had left my employer and gone independent. She inquired what I was doing. When I explained, she proclaimed, "If you are going to be speaking in front of winners, you must have a company name!" I thought about it and that night I went home and referred to the dictionary. When I read the definition of "boost" I knew that was what I wanted to do for businesses and HRBoost™ became my Limited Liability Corporation. For years, I enjoyed consulting and though my practice had a couple of employees, I never regarded myself as "in business." I truly was living my ministry, workplace ministry. So many businesses needed to reframe the way they treated their employees.

My first Managed Service client had successfully grown from 10 million to 26 million and HRBoost was the retained provider during those growth years. One primary objective was to create a Best and Brightest® workplace. We achieved this in partnership with our client within the first 12 months. It was then that I realized it was not magic. I realized I had a process. Even so, I still viewed myself as a consultant. From 2011 to 2013, we retained this client and successfully partnered with them through due diligence and acquisition. The business sold for $58 million. During the transition of the business, a key executive approached me. I had worked with this individual for years and we had become friends. To my surprise, one day he said to me, "Nicole, I really like your business!" I thanked him of course but he went on to say, "I would like to invest in your business. I could offer you a $100,000." I replied with some reluctance and stated, "I am a consultant!" He replied, "No, you are in business!"

## I Am Sorry, You See Me As Who?

I was stunned. He was serious! I went home and told my husband what had happened. His response was less than favorable. That was the day I learned that I could not talk to him about business. As he saw it, this was another man offering me money – and for what? He must want something. He must have some hidden agenda. I knew that was not true. Either way, I knew I could never accept his offer. How could I? I declined graciously, and we kept in contact. I was experiencing tremendous growth in my business, all through word-of mouth-referrals. I felt the business was running me vs. me running the business.

About that time, a client asked me if I had heard of the Goldman Sachs "10,000 Small Businesses" program. I said, "I am just a little consulting firm." He continued, "Well, do you have four employees? Have you been in business for three years? Do you have at least $150,000 in revenue for each of those years?" Indeed, I answered "yes" to all three questions. He said, "Then you should apply!" I reviewed the program online, and it seemed to be just what I needed. The process was rigorous. I submitted all my financial data and completed an application. I was selected for an interview, and in 2014, I was accepted into the program through the City College in Chicago. This was a 16-week intensive course in which you work through modules to complete your five-year business plan, complete with financial modeling. When I began the program, I recall being asked to write down my vision for my business and then sealing it in an envelope. I remember writing, "I would like to have a million-dollar consulting firm!" At the completion of the program, after I completed my business plan and my five-year forecast, I opened the envelope to reflect on my growth. I was struck with emotion – I literally began crying in the classroom. Not only did I overcome fear by learning, but I saw for the first time what that man who had offered me a $100,000 investment had seen in me just a year before. My business had the potential to be five times what I had originally forecast.

## Overcoming Fear

After founding my business in 2010, it was a full five years before I realized I was actually *in business*. By January 1, 2015, I had entered into a partnership agreement with an investor. The difference now was that when I did this, I knew what I was giving up, and I knew the value of it. I also was empowered to fully execute the terms of the agreement to ensure that my interests were protected. I had taken the time to truly understand the opportunity, the financials, and the benchmark data. As a result, I felt prepared for the discussion rather than being naïve and, as result, I was empowered and no longer afraid of the unknown. After all, *I was in business*. I just did not realize it until I had a business plan in front of me.

Today, I can say that I have built a successful and profitable business doing what I love. I consider myself an "accidental entrepreneur," but it is amazing what transpires when we allow ourselves to evolve into who we are meant to become. I now have 15 employees and hundreds of clients. If you had told me 10 years ago that I would be doing what I am doing now, I would not have believed you. In fact, I would never have devoted time to writing if it had not been for my business attorney who first invited me to contribute a chapter to a book back in 2014.

Often, we fail to see what others see in us. There is a whole field of psychology devoted to these "metaperceptions." Ultimately, we strive to learn what others think of us and, yet, we can understand how they see us only when *we* can see ourselves as clearly. I never believed I would be a successful businesswoman – until I was. I never believed I would be a successful author – until I was. Think of times you have been complimented only to shrug it off. What about you do others see that *you* disregard?

Once I realized that I have gifts, I have been committed to sharing them. Everyone has a gift – something special and unique. When we are young, our parents view us as special and unique, but then we become adults and somehow our self-perceptions turn to average and, in some cases, worse. I had to overcome fear to get to this place.

I remember being afraid of getting more business. The high growth I experienced early on in my business was challenging. I had 50% growth year-over-year in the beginning, and it was scary. I used to fear upsetting some player in the industry, especially when I would find my business going head-to-head against a much bigger business in the proposal stage. I would think, "I am not competing against them." It was as if I did not want to ruffle feathers or impose on someone else's territory, while really, it was solely stemming from my fear of failure. What if quality suffered? What if I stretched myself too thin? How could I afford the six-figure talent needed to get to the next level? I had growth numbers that others would die for, but I found myself working more than when I had my corporate job – and making less. I started my business with less than $1,000. For five years, I invested every dollar I earned into the business. When I finally did the benchmarks, I realized I needed to be charging more. I have found that I always learn the hard way. When I took the time to really understand my own numbers, I found that I had not priced myself properly to cover for SG&A (Selling, General, and Administrative Expenses – a major non-production cost). I was working so hard, but I was in the red. If I had quit then, I would never be where I am now.

In making every critical decision to date, I knew it was my truth and my calling. I knew I loved what I was doing, and I was determined to overcome the many obstacles. I knew many men who were very successful. The more I reflected on these men and their skills, the more I asked myself, "How hard can it really be? If *they* can do this, *I* can do this." Then, further doubts came into play. As a mother, I worried about how much I was working, especially in 2013 as I built the infrastructure and searched for qualified talent. Many women I know are successful and some are entrepreneurial, but most were business-to-business rather than business-to-customer. Often, their children were grown. Others were career women by choice, and I presume sacrifices were made. I wanted more. I figured that if you are independent and leading your business, you should be able to flex your schedule to meet your needs. That is easier said than done, however. I still craved the ability to achieve work/life *integration* – forget work/life *balance*. I needed to identify what gives me joy and how I could structure that in my life. At the same time, I identified what drains me and is necessary but must be managed.

I listened to my intuition and was faithful to what I knew to be true. Sometimes, just knowing what is *wrong* for you is the key to knowing what is *right*. I remember a time when others told me I could not do what I was actually doing. The reality is that I always believed in myself at each step, and every engagement was my personal ministry to heal the workplace. When I did not feel confident, I sought to learn more. I did not dream big, but I can say that at each step, I knew I was doing what was right for me at that time. I once read that "fear is the cheapest room in the house."[7] It is a daily practice to feel your truth, moment to moment, to acknowledge your fears and meet them head on. I always imagine the worst, and once I come to terms of what that may be, I proceed. To quit or give up would leave me feeling regretful or as though I did not fully live. I would not have the thought it if it were not meant to be. I truly believe the inspiration that comes in the peaceful moments while the world sleeps is meant to be acted upon.

It is commitment to faith to live your truth moment to moment. To be truly present and mindful, you must commit to authentically being true to yourself, loving yourself as a child of God. Jon Kabat-Zinn has spoken that mindfulness is the gateway into the full dimensionality of your spirituality[8]. By loving yourself enough to project love to others, you become authentically *you*. Without pause, we can do what we have always done. I encourage you to pause, be with your emotions, and feel your intuition speaking to you. When you are truly present with your thoughts and emotions, you can begin to hear the voice of intuition clearly. Ask yourself, "Could this be my place of belonging? Can I lift my vibration to what I want to experience?"

Spiritually, we cannot *have* what we have not *become*. I knew I had to lift my vibration to radiate positive energy to another person. To keep it, I must believe it and be it. Otherwise, it is fleeting. The key to joy is finding it within you. Your joy does not reside within another human being – it is sourced from your deepest self, your Spirit, your life force.

Being yourself is the greatest challenge we all bear. I remember when my mother moved to live closer to me many years ago. It is a fact that the Midwest is slightly more conservative than the West. She was raised in California and lived in Montana for many years as well. I always joke that there are three types of people back home – the independently wealthy, those who own business and ranch the land, and those who just do not give a damn. My mother has always been 100% herself, and she does not live to anyone's expectations but her own. When I was younger, I remember projecting on her. For example, my mother is so free and comfortable in her own skin that she can run about town without wearing a bra. This embarrassed me often when I was young. Finally, one day she said, "I am comfortable this way, and if it bothers others, so be it. But I do not need to do it for them or for you!" She was right. I was projecting a self-imposed societal expectation on her, and who was I to do that? That was *my* issue, not hers. The fact that she can be herself at all times is truly a gift. If only we could all be so fortunate. I think it may be the strongest example I can learn from. Many of us are not that self-confident, including myself. Loving yourself is the greatest gift. I suppose I will feel that I am living that fully when I do not self-judge my imperfections against any external standard. The challenge remains that our own standards can often leave us competing against ourselves.

I have no idea what the future holds. Nobody does. Clarity is not the objective. But being true to our values, our beliefs, and our gifts, is the only path to be the person God intended – authentically. I have sought prayer and communion with God regularly throughout my life. I especially needed it when my husband and I were expecting our second son in the spring of 2018. I had to ask myself, "How can my business run without me for three months?" I wanted to take maternity leave, but the first person to ask me how I would do this was my husband! I told him, "It will work itself out!" and, just like that, I threw it up to God. I met the woman who would replace me in the field literally two weeks before I gave birth to my new son.

There is something very sacred about welcoming a child home. Maybe it was hormones or the fact that I knew this child would be my last, but I took those three months and relied on my team to do what I knew they could do. When I returned to meet with clients during renewal, I learned that not only did we deliver on brand promise, but the clients were happy. When I saw that the business not only survived but finished in the black that year, I knew I had done more than grow *personally*, I had grown *professionally*.

I still pray and seek guidance before making important decisions, and often, my greatest act of faith is simply letting go, living in gratitude, and striving to live with presence. I may never get clarity, but at this very moment I grasp it, trust it, and with faith, I move forward. I see myself on a spiritual journey. Believing that others are doing this as well is the key to living in kindness and generosity. To live authentically is to regard others in their authenticity as well. How we grace one another and teach one another is breathtaking when you truly reflect on it. Each moment I live, I aim to live in service. Perhaps it is subtle. Sometimes I step forward, and other times, I step backward. The grace is knowing when to do what while committing to move through fear and hesitation to experience bliss and wonder, finding yourself in the quiet space of the opportunity of this moment. Trust it. Become your dreams realized!

# ———— YOUR DREAMS REALIZED ————

*May this visioning exercise take you through a reflective journey to see your dreams clearly. To live with joy and purpose in your day, it must begin with vision. There is no right way to go about this. It need not be perfect. And it is only a dreaming exercise, so release your fears!*

## *Imagine if you could ...*

**Complete your own Circle of Life diagram:**

1. Consider the 10 areas of life categories and think briefly what an ideal life might look like for you to feel joyful, content and purposeful in each category.

2. Next, draw a line across the diagram that represents your level of joy presently for each category. It is important to go with the first rating value that comes to your mind. Not the number you think it should be but the real number you feel today.

3. Imagine the center of your Life diagram is 0 and the outer edges are 10.

4. Choose a value between 1 (*NO JOY*) and 10 (*JOYFUL*).

**Now draw a line and write the numeric value alongside your line.**

**How do you balance these areas of your life?**

| | | | | | | | | | | |
|---|---|---|---|---|---|---|---|---|---|---|
| (Family) | 1 | 2 | 3 | 4 | 5 | 6 | 7 | 8 | 9 | 10 |
| (Playtime) | 1 | 2 | 3 | 4 | 5 | 6 | 7 | 8 | 9 | 10 |
| (Profession) | 1 | 2 | 3 | 4 | 5 | 6 | 7 | 8 | 9 | 10 |
| (Spiritual Health) | 1 | 2 | 3 | 4 | 5 | 6 | 7 | 8 | 9 | 10 |
| (Contribution) | 1 | 2 | 3 | 4 | 5 | 6 | 7 | 8 | 9 | 10 |
| (Health) | 1 | 2 | 3 | 4 | 5 | 6 | 7 | 8 | 9 | 10 |
| (Intimacy/Relationships) | 1 | 2 | 3 | 4 | 5 | 6 | 7 | 8 | 9 | 10 |
| (Financial Security) | 1 | 2 | 3 | 4 | 5 | 6 | 7 | 8 | 9 | 10 |
| (Social) | 1 | 2 | 3 | 4 | 5 | 6 | 7 | 8 | 9 | 10 |
| (Personal Growth) | 1 | 2 | 3 | 4 | 5 | 6 | 7 | 8 | 9 | 10 |

**Now Plot your numbers and categories on the Circle of Life Diagram:**

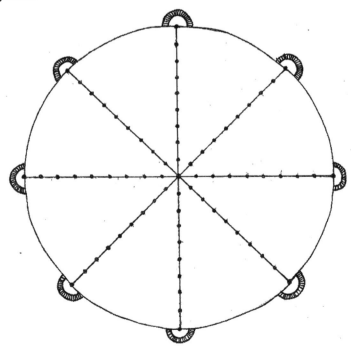

A regular check in with your Circle of Life diagram is recommended. If you find this difficult, ask a close friend to complete the reflection with you. Sometimes it is helpful to see an outside perspective on your life balance. This person must be someone you trust and ideally, they will love you as you are. They will speak truth out of love.

## Answer and reflect on these questions:

What if you could do anything for yourself, for YOU? What would that be?

_____

_____

### Detailed Reflections:

Now state an ideal around each with a value in mind. What do you value around each life category and what does it look like ideally for you at its most *JOYFUL?*

_____

_____

## What would it look like to feel fully *JOYFUL*?

| Value | Present Reality | Ideal Vision |
|---|---|---|
| **Family** | | |
| Home | | |
| *Family* | | |
| *Extended Family* | | |
| *Soul Family* | | |
| **Playtime** | | |
| Recreation | | |
| **Profession** | | |
| *Work* | | |
| *Motherhood* | | |
| *Business* | | |
| *Caregiver* | | |
| **Spiritual Health** | | |
| Faith in Practice | | |
| *Meditation* | | |
| *Relaxation* | | |
| *Private Time* | | |
| **Contribution** | | |
| Service | | |
| *Gratitude Exercises* | | |
| *Volunteering* | | |
| *Charity* | | |

| Value | Present Reality | Ideal Vision |
|---|---|---|
| **Health** | | |
| Fitness | | |
| *Mental Health* | | |
| *Physical Health* | | |
| *Emotional Health* | | |
| *Physical Strength* | | |
| **Intimacy/ Relationships** | | |
| Dating | | |
| *Relationships* | | |
| *Life Partner* | | |
| *Love* | | |
| **Financial Security** | | |
| Money | | |
| *Finances* | | |
| *Financial Wellbeing* | | |
| **Social** | | |
| Friends | | |
| *Clubs* | | |
| *Groups* | | |
| **Personal Growth** | | |
| Self-Development | | |
| *Learning* | | |
| *Growing* | | |

**Now look at what you wrote down. Consider these reflections**

Are there any surprises?

_____

_____

How do you feel about your life as you look at the complete Circle of Life diagram?

_____

_____

Which of these categories would you most like to devote your time and energy to bringing back in balance?

_____

_____

How can you make space for these changes?

_____

_____

What help and support might you need from others to increase the JOY in your life?

_____

_____

What change should you make first?

_____

_____

What change do you want to make first?

_____

_____

If there was one key action you could take that would begin to bring everything into purposeful view, what would it be?

_____

_____

What is the smallest step you can begin with?

_____

_____

**Now imagine if resources were not a limiting factor**

Imagine if you had $50,000 given to you today. What would you do differently?

_____

_____

Now, imagine if you had $500,000 given to you today. What would you do differently? Would your vision change if you had a $1 million?

_____

_____

How did your thinking change when limiting resources, such as money, was not a factor? Reflect on your vision when you had no financial limitations. What would you do differently?

_____

_____

Lock into that vision and begin to build a bridge to the possibilities of your dreams realized. To live your dreams, you must first vision them.

_____

_____

If your vision does not change with added resources, then you know you are living your dreams. Often our dreams are right before us seeking our *presence.*

_____

_____

What areas were out of balance?

_____

_____


What strategies can you put into place to help you fill your soul cup? Sometimes, the most spontaneous act can fill your soul cup. Other times, it will be the consistent commitment to working towards the vision. Remember, the vision is for YOU!

_____

_____


Who do you want to be?

_____

_____


What do you want to be remembered for?

_____

_____

# PRESENCE PRINCIPLE 6
## *Surround Yourself*

*"There can be no happiness if the things we believe in are different from the things we do."*

−FREYA STARK

## Defining Happiness

I do not know where I was or exactly when it occurred. It was not a magnificent, memorable moment that I recall with clarity. It seems odd, as everything to date had a milestone to it. I just know that one day I woke up and I felt truly happy – deeply content and for the first time, perhaps ever, I knew that just being in "this moment" was enough. Perhaps I had finally stopped focusing on what I was doing and I was suddenly more present in what I was becoming. I had connected to a deeper meaning in my day. With my dreams realized, I had come to a joyful realization that being the mother I had always wanted to be did not mean I had to change who I was. It did not mean that I had to stop growing or put off my dreams and just live vicariously through my child. Rather, I felt fully alive.

By 2013, my business was growing at a high rate – literally, at 50%. Despite knowing the importance of balance, it did not take long to feel the consequences of growth. As they say, be careful what you wish for! Most people think that when you own business, you can choose your hours. I have found that when you own your own business, it is never fully out of your mind.

I remember a time when my number-one client was my first-born child. That all changed when my husband elected to retire early. One day, he just asked me, "What would you think if I stayed home with our son?" It took me a minute to understand what he was proposing. I was raised by a single mother, and I do not know that I truly believed people actually *retired*, and certainly not in their forties! Yet, he was serious. In that moment, I realized that my sole purpose in marriage was to support my husband in his passions, just as he supports me with mine. And so, he became the primary caregiver and I devoted more of my energy to what I once called "my second baby," HRBoost! With freedom and stability at home, I fully immersed my mind with my newfound passion. I called it "workplace ministry," and before long, I had doubled my revenue in less than seven days! That is when I realized that my business was, in fact, more than *me*.

As I continued on this journey, it is no surprise that I was juggling. All mothers juggle. I began to feel out of balance. I thought I had boundaries, and yet, in retrospect, I may not have dropped any of my responsibilities. I felt exhausted. I found myself struggling to get home in time for dinner. It was not just a busy month – it was a busy year. At the end of that year, I asked myself, "Is this what I really wanted?" The answer was *no*. I was in reactive mode, people-pleasing, saying "yes!" to everyone, and not recognizing what really was important. It is easy to get off course, and I concluded that if I could not control my schedule to protect the things that were important to me, then it was not worth it. I gave myself a year to challenge myself and see if I could perfect work/life integration to the satisfaction of my family, my employees, my clients, and myself.

## Knowing When To Say No!

I joined a CEO peer group to help me regain the rigor of working "on" my business. I will never forget my first exchange with them. At the time, this group made up of a few successful men who led businesses ranging from $1 million to $10 million in revenue. They asked me what I did, and when I told them, they laughed and said things like, "I feel lazy!" and "I feel exhausted!"

As I got to know them, I realized that I was doing a fairly big number of things, and perhaps I had failed to realize that some of those tasks did not align with my new purpose. My first task was to establish criteria for the things I would say "yes" to, which essentially became the criteria for the things I say "no" to. After I reconciled everything to this new criterion, I began making the transition to aligning what I *did* with who I had *become*. Declining offers and saying "no" can be harder than it sounds. In some cases, I had to resign from boards I had served on and other non-essential groups. Many of the things I had been doing were enjoyable but were not contributing to my top priorities at the time. Once I had the criteria in my mind and determined to align my activities to those criteria, it became easier to say no. It became more about protecting my *presence* and overall well-being, and that included being home for dinner and unplugging on weekends.

I reviewed my values. Instead of just *having* them, I tied metrics to them. I asked myself how was I protecting my time and energy. It was not enough to just *say* what I wanted – I had to carve out time for each thing that was important to my definition of success. "Success" included gym time, date nights, family vacation time, work-from-home days, time with my sons both together and one on one, and more. If I could not have those things, *nothing* was worth it – not the business, the money, or the achievements.

For the first time, I made a deliberate choice to guard my private time, protect my energy, and know when to leave my office – and in contrast, know when to leave my home. I remember when I did not know how to say no without feeling as if I had let someone down or passed on a rewarding opportunity. It was as if I had to give up one thing that seemed important only to sacrifice another thing that seemed equally important, when in fact, that was not the case at all. I was giving up what was no longer in alignment with my sole purpose and my ideal environment for optimal *presence*.

It is amazing what happens when you commit not only your physical presence but your mental *presence* and align them to support and reinforce your passion and purpose. By embracing the change that was upon me, I found a new way to make it all happen. I believe I have perfected the art of compartmentalization through my commitment to *presence*. Sure, it is a daily challenge but I have committed to a structure that supports the desired outcomes. I aim to give 100% of myself to any given moment, whether that moment is with my son, my husband, my business, my clients, my trainer, or anyone else. Sometimes I feel rushed but I make a point to apologize for that when it happens. By isolating my thoughts and energy in any given moment, I protect *presence*. By defining metrics for each value, I aim to uphold, I have confidence in knowing that, from moment to moment, I have not forsaken any that were important because I devoted my time to each one respectively.

## Together, Everyone Achieves More

In the years that followed, my business continued to expand. And as life goes, blessings make themselves known. In 2015, my husband and I were expecting our second child. This time, I had new obligations that I could not just walk away from. Ironically, I never worried. I felt such joy in my heart, and I simply *knew* all would work itself out. Yes, I have faith, and lots of it! Just two weeks before the arrival of our second son, I hired my first senior-level consultant (the woman who would replace me in the field). I had done everything necessary to lock in the team and the right number of clients. This allowed me to take maternity leave.

As I said before, when you have your own business, you never really turn it off and, truly, I was engaged – but on an intermittent basis. I did not actually meet with anyone for about three months. I knew I would never get this time back again. I feel that God gave me a tremendous gift, both then and now. There is nothing more special than a child, and I cannot think of anything other than a newborn that would have allowed me to do what many entrepreneurs fail to do ... to let go. I had to trust that my team knew their craft and our brand promise and that the work processed that were in place would be enough.

When I returned from leave and met with the clients, I was ready to hear their feedback and see the numbers. To my delight, not only did our key clients renew their annual agreements, but they were quite pleased with our team's performance. The business finished in the black and with improved profitability. I cried when I saw the year-end results! It had taken eight years in business to learn how to work less and achieve more ... as a *team!* Yet, I could never have let go long enough, trusted enough, and delegated enough to test this if not for my beautiful newborn son, a team of dedicated professionals, and God (of course). Today, I like to ask some of my peer business owners, "If you left your business for three months, what would happen?"

## Protecting Presence

Life is ever-changing. As you live your dreams and increase your success, it will become even more important to protect your time and energy. If you have successfully worked through the foundational *Principles for Presence,* you will surround yourself with all the framework needed to sustain your joy, reinforce your purpose, and protect your environment. The first thing to do is check your emotions and stay in touch with how you truly feel. Next, verify that your expectations align with your passion, calling, and purpose. Reconcile your top priorities with actionable steps or metrics so you can hold yourself accountable. Last, control your environment for optimal presence.

You deserve a sanctuary space. You have a right to not always be "on," social, and outward-facing. Surround your home with things that enhance your personal sanctuary. Make it a place where you can escape. Invest in your space so you can delight in it. Sometimes, small items such as a rubbing stone, a candle, or music streaming in the background can protect your frame of mind and your presence. I personally love essential oil diffusers and visual items that inspire me. If my children are giggling and jumping around, I will brew herbal tea any time of the day or night. Yesterday, I found great comfort in throwing my sweater in the dryer before putting it on. Remember the trivial things that bring you back to *you* in an instant. Being present with what works for you is so important because we cannot always control our environment. Often, chaos can enter our space. The challenge is to stay centered and peaceful despite what our conscious mind witnesses around us.

At times, you may find yourself out of balance, feeling depleted, anxious, or perhaps even nurturing emotions of guilt or self-doubt. These can creep up despite your best efforts, so you must first acknowledge how you feel. Sometimes it is hard to just admit when something is not working for you. Make it your goal to find the source of the imbalance. In what area did you fall out of sync? When we do not make it a practice to pause and acknowledge how we feel, we can push ourselves too far, even to the point of illness.

Our conscious minds are wired to respond to what we see and hear, but we often forget that our subconscious mind holds all our experiences, feelings, memories, and intentions. Think of your conscious mind's priority – to make sense of all that comes at you. These days, that is a full-time job! The conscious mind can only do so much without your subconscious mind telling it what to do. The subconscious mind will prioritize any internal imbalance over the conscious mind regardless if your conscious mind is dealing with external stimulation.

When I was working full-time and completing my graduate degree, I took each day as it came, one at a time. I felt tired, I was depleted, and I was not taking care of myself. I was eating fast food, not sleeping well, and I missed my home. Honestly, between work and my schooling, I am lucky that my husband was still there after those two grueling years! This was only a few months after Brian and I married. My mother had moved to Illinois and I enjoyed all the nurturing things she did for me.

I remember rushing to final presentations one semester after work. I was thinking positive, affirming thoughts while reciting my presentation in my head. I felt ready – in fact, I felt excited! All was good in my world ... or so I thought in my conscious mind. When I got out of my car, I felt a sharp pain in my stomach. I practically bent over and set my bag down. I paused and prayed, "Not now!" My subconscious mind had prioritized my wellness over my conscious mind's priorities. I had not been good to myself, and neglecting self-care has consequences.

I somehow managed to get through my presentation, but I drove myself to the emergency room right after class. It was the night before Thanksgiving and I needed to see a specialist. I was admitted because no one sees a specialist on Thanksgiving unless you are in the hospital. Days later, I was told I had gastritis. All that ibuprofen I had taken for my arthritic pain on an empty stomach had stripped my stomach lining. My gastroenterologist said I would be better off taking a gentle prescription instead. In fact, he said, "Unless you want to die from stomach cancer, you will never take ibuprofen again!" Needless to say, he got my attention. This painful example clearly shows how our subconscious works for us even when we do not.

The nature of "busy" can keep us from being present. Unrealistic expectations may be at the source. In my case, I have certainly been guilty of taking on too many creative projects. Not until I learned to begin with the end in mind could I connect my daily commitments to my values and anticipated results. For example, I expect intimacy in my marriage. Now, with all I do outside my home and with two young children, this requires diligence! To achieve this, I aim to give two days a week (every other day) back to my husband by working from home. This also allows me to spend time with our young son, working around his naps. This intentional rhythm for the week supports both my husband and me. I am blessed to have family nearby, so we make efforts to include overnight date nights every month. We make it a point to escape for a weekend every quarter and for annual four- or five-day vacations, just the two of us. I expect to be close with my sons. To me, "close" means open conversations (no question is off limits), "peak and pit" reviews, and daily prayer. Moments like these bring me back to my breath and my gratitude. When I am truly present in it, time stands still.

I audit myself regularly. I intentionally carve out time to devote my energy to the values that mean the most to me and to consider how I would want to be regarded if I died tomorrow. In fact, on any day when I do not feel balance – work, home, family, fun, social, and self – I adapt my environment to bring myself back to a place of peaceful *presence*.

Now, not every balance inequity requires a full recalibration. Knowing yourself is the key to realizing whether you need to completely review what you are doing versus who you are becoming. Once you master this, you may find little ways to bring yourself back to a state of being present. To just *be* is the goal. To be and feel *joyful* contentment, with no distraction or being somewhere else in your mind – or worse, feeling so tired that you have nothing left to give. *Joy* is not sourced from a commitment to excellence. *Joy* is sourced from love – unconditional love of ourselves and those around us. As *yourself*, think of ways to grow in a capacity of love so you can *give* love. Belonging is key to feeling loved, but we must first love and nurture ourselves in order to radiate love and *joy* to others.

As I am writing this, I have come up to a number of deadlines (including finishing this manuscript). Of course, I reserve time to write, but billable clients are often slipped into writing times. Whether I am writing in my dream journal, my family journal, a blog or creative project, I need complete space and a blank canvas in my mind. Reaching a state of presence and calm in my mind is essential. God's grace allows me to quiet my conscious mind and hear my subconscious mind.

So, what do I do? I wake early each morning and set my intention for the day. I keep a journal appropriately named the *Make It Happen!* Journal[9] While I have tons of color-coded tasks and emails, this journal becomes my focused place for what *must* happen today. I am old-school ... I still like paper and printed books. I reflect on what I must do to be successful, and then I ease into it before my children wake.

I also have a dream journal where I write down creative thoughts. We all get those fleeting thoughts from our dreams or in moments where our mind is still enough to hear the subconscious mind. I always jot those things down and circle back to them when I can actually be present with them. I feel giddy when I have something to look forward to as I process my own meditative thoughts.

From a practical standpoint, I am better when I begin my day this way. I never thought I would be a morning person, but I have certainly become one. Often, I watch the sunrise; nothing is more breathtaking. As I spur my positive energy into action, I review the day with my husband so we're both prepared each day. After all, this is a "we" operation!

Throughout the day, I drink herbal teas and moisturize my hands with Aveda Stress Fix. Something as simple as this allows me to place my hands over my nose and mouth and deeply breathe an aroma that instantly brings me to a place of peace and presence. I turn off my ringers and email notifications when I need to focus solely on the list that *must* happen today. If something takes me away from my family, I will be home in time for dinner. I have a date night with my older son this month, a Mommy and Me class with my younger son yet this week, solace with my husband post-bedtime each night, and plans with a girlfriend within the month. By making sure that my calendar matches my intentions, I allow myself greater *presence* moment to moment.

This practice has squelched any anxiety that once would have been lurking such feelings of guilt, or questions of how I can manage it all. I've embraced faith to empower my belief that God puts before us what we need to evolve. Knowing that I've devoted time to protect what matters to me gives me energy and peace of mind. By protecting the practices and time that energizes me, I have more to give to others.

My schedule includes doing things I do not like. For example, I do not enjoy hard exercise. And let us be honest – unless you are an athlete, it is all hard! I have a love/hate relationship with it. Living with physical pain for most of my life, I have learned that exercise is the one thing I *must* do to evade pain. I know I might avoid back surgery one day due to my herniated discs if I strengthen my core. I wish I could say I invested in a trainer for my vanity, but the truth is far from it. I work out with a trainer up to three times a week so I can run in heels, lift my two-year-old when he is struggling to get down, and challenge myself to grow in ways that would be nearly impossible without my trainer. I am sure to let her know the gift she is to me. It is my spirit striving to overcome. Working with a trainer is actually more affordable than my health insurance premiums and the medical expenses if I do not take care of my overall health.

Every now and then, give yourself a spontaneous and indulgent gift. I miss Montana, and while I appreciate the best of both worlds, I live in an urban environment. This past year, I packed up my family and flew to Glacier Park in Montana for three days. Yes, it was a splurge, but you know what? It filled my soul cup more than I ever imagined. Sometimes, you just need to do things like that. *Joy* is sourced from realizing the opportunity in every moment.

PRESENCE TOOLS 6

## REINFORCING PRESENCE

*May this recalibration exercise take you through a reflective exercise to ensure you are protecting your time and your energy to live with presence.*

*To live with presence through all the ebbs and flow of life, we need reinforcements and prayer reflection. Committing to self-care and self-love is critical to sustaining the right balance so you can remain loving and generous to others. What strategies, practices and resources will keep your soul cup full?*

## Create a safe place for reflection: Emotions

Emotions are at the core of *presence*. Which practices do you need to stay present with your emotions, your heart, and your breath? Let stillness be your guide. Some people find peace in physical practices like yoga, hiking outdoors, or Pilates. Others escape to the seashore, lakes, or oceans to be near the water. Journaling can quiet the mind and help identify your inner voice and habitual patterns. Whatever your preferred practice, be sure you protect the path that keeps you in sync with your emotions. Never forget how you are feeling, and remember to nurture your heart and pulse your emotions. Honor your emotions. You are the only person who can give yourself permission to be happy.

Anxiety rises to the surface when you have to make a decision. You may be facing something new or different, or trying to avoid something difficult. If you carry guilt and try to do more than is humanly possible, you must realize that only you can choose guilt. It is "B." You can change "B." Remember, it is your choice. No one is perfect. We are all flawed. Feel your emotions. Feel and heal. You can turn any negative emotion into an invitation, an opportunity to grow.

**List the ways in which you honor your emotions, and identify your preferred way to quiet your mind, release your stress behaviors, and truly feel your emotions (subconscious).**

---

---

## Create a place that is your sanctuary: Environment

We often forget that we can control our responses. We may not be able to always control our *environment*. What we allow in is up to us. Often, others come into our spaces. Find ways to maintain spaces that you call your own and infuse images, items, and scents that comfort you. Center your mind to a place of *presence*. For some, images can bring peace; for others, it is subtle fragrances, natural elements like plants, flowers, or essential oil diffusers. Special adaptations can include lighting, music, even color. Whatever brings you to a place of comfort, peace, and safety must be upheld. Protect your time so you can enjoy being in your sanctuary space. If you cannot find it in your home, find a place outside or some other place of spiritual retreat to replenish your senses. Create your environment and protect your time so you are able to retreat to your sanctuary whenever you need to recharge, pause, breathe, rethink, or replenish. **List the ways you create a sanctuary for yourself. How can you make your environment a sanctuary for your soul?**

_____

_____

## Meditate to set your intention: Expectations and Desires

When we rush through our days, we can lose our focus. As a result, we lose our sense of _presence_. Each day is meant to begin with your intention. Some people wake early to allow a gradual awakening to take place. Others have a peaceful practice in the evening to lead into the coming day. Breathe, pause, and be sure that your intentions are in the forefront of your mind. You can breathe light and color into your meditation – blue for calm, green for healing, pink for youthfulness and vitality, and yellow for mental clarity. If you find your intentions veering off course, forgive yourself and breathe. Reflect on how you are feeling. Take the time needed to align your intentions with how you would like to feel. When you are off course, build ways to protect your intentions. We need to let go of expectations and open our hearts and minds to what is before us _right now, in this moment_. What is your intention in this moment? All we have is this moment, so breathe it in and come to it with _presence_. **Identify your expectations and connect them to your intentions. Do they align with this present moment?**

_____

_____

# PRESENCE PRINCIPLES 7
## *Finding Purpose*

*"Healing may not be so much about getting better as
about letting go of everything that is not you – all of the
expectations, all of the beliefs – and becoming who you are."*

–RACHEL NAOMI REMEN

## Do People Have A Calling?

Growing up in a small town, I never knew all that the world had to offer. My mother always instilled "possibilities," but in retrospect, I realize that there are people who take joy in things I could never do. Surely, they are pursuing their passions. Some are fortunate to know their passion early in life. They come alive in their uniqueness early. Others live for other people's passions – perhaps their parents' expectations or something they told themselves they must do, only to find in midlife that their lives had little to do with their passion.

I believe passion is invigorating. It propels us to pursue it even when we fail, despite what others feel is right for us. No matter the consequence, passion emerges from the depths of our Spirit. Passion is who we are, who we are meant to be. If it is truly sourced from Christ Consciousness, we find that we naturally connect our passion to impact that of another human being ... to give it away, to make someone else's life better.

My mother taught me something that took me many years to understand. She works to live, versus lives to work. She intentionally lives with less to truly live. As a healer, the way she protects her time and energy has been quite an example for me. Of course, there are others who channel their passion to the benefit themselves. That can be energy-depleting, and unless the intrinsic intention is connected to your life's purpose, your calling, and your passion, it will be empty. There is a delicate balance, and true purpose is subtle. It is the underlying layer. To be in touch with our subconscious mind, we stretch to grow and learn beyond the status quo, not to achieve an award or a pay raise, but to expand our hearts and minds to a higher state of being spiritually, emotionally, and physically.

Passion is not a job. It is the fuel that powers you to *do* the job. Purpose is the outcome when your passion takes you to a place of transcendence, whereby you can see and feel how your uniqueness can contribute to the greater good. Perhaps not on a global scale but in *this* room for *this* person in *this* moment, you have raised the vibration to a level of sovereignty that resonates. We are all gifts to one another in a greater system. The challenge is to realize how you are unique and, in turn, coming to an awareness of your God-given gifts is a blessing.

I used to take it for granted that I felt comfortable in ambiguous situations. I once thought everyone in my field thought the way I did. I even believed that we all executed the work in my field in a similar fashion. My husband would like to think that everyone keeps a home as meticulously as ours. Only through me has he come to know that I see him as a beautiful gift to me and our boys.

Being aware of your gift is the first step in sourcing your calling, whatever you can do better than anyone else. Perhaps you take it for granted. Do not! It's your gift. Consider how you can channel that gift into a form of service. When you find the way to live the gift in service, it becomes a passion that others feel and receive, and that can truly become your purpose. I believe we all have a calling. I believe we hear it deep within our subconscious minds. Whether we acknowledge it with our conscious mind and become present with it, will determine whether *presence* fuels your *joy* and your purpose.

I have never seen myself as a healer. My mother is a healer, without question. But I have learned one thing about purpose: Our gifts can in fact become our passions. Our strengths are enacted through our behaviors. The critical choice, however, is giving it away. I have learned that we are not meant to use our gifts on ourselves. And in many cases, I have come to believe that we *cannot*.

My brother has become a nurturing healer in his own right. He is a tier-two paramedic. I glanced at his textbooks once. He is smarter than I am, for sure! And so easy-going! To stay calm in crisis is a gift, and to impart that calm security to someone in a vulnerable state is truly incredible. Sometimes, it takes others to reflect to us what makes us uniquely special. At other times, we can find it is with us all along.

For my whole life, I have been my mother's daughter. Even though my mother was single, I never wondered where my daddy was. My mother provided all I could ever want or need, and she was so young and playful that my childhood was wonderful. Early in my life, I suppose we had conversations about this, but I have no recollection. I grew up with an understanding that my father had died. With no memories of him, I never questioned it. I remember how hard my mother worked, and I was definitely a latchkey kid. Her work ethic surely rubbed off on me. We all reflect on our childhood, and I seem to romanticize mine to some degree. My glass-half-full perspective is innate, and perhaps I was naïve. I never had a father presence in my life until my mother married when I was 15. By then, I spent so much time with school and work that I never established a strong bond with my stepfather. It was not until I was a young woman on my own that I could understand that my mother had her own life and deserved companionship beyond her children. Having been an only child for some time before my brother came along, I had become accustomed to having my mother for myself.

## It Comes Through You

I was 18 years old and living in Illinois. I had been away from my family for nearly a year. It was spring or summer, as I recall, and late at night. I was already in bed when the phone rang. It was a man. He identified himself and called me by my nickname, Niki. He said, "Niki, this is your daddy."

I think my mind went into shock. I knew this man, but only as a name on my birth certificate. When I moved out of state, my mother provided my "essential documents," and a man named Carl Cornwell was listed as my father on my birth certificate. My mother had always told me that Carl was *not* my father, and that he was a man named Leonard, and I had accepted it. I trusted my mother, and she had never lied to me. I could feel her heart when she discussed this with me, and I was confident it was her truth. Over the years, she had never changed her story. She always explained that Leonard died unexpectedly in a motorcycle accident, and when she spoke of him, I knew he was the love of her life. My mother always said that Carl was there when I was born and took care of her. He had a job with good insurance, and he offered to put me on his insurance – but he was not my father. That was always the story, and it was enough for me.

Well, it was until Carl called. I wondered how he had gotten my phone number. I was silent, and he continued, "I know we do not have a relationship and you do not know me. I have settled down and made my life right. I am married and have two children with my wife, Linda – a daughter and a son with special needs." About this time, my boyfriend started getting annoyed because I was on the phone. He asked me who I was talking to. I did not know what to say. My boyfriend became agitated and started yelling as I continued to listen to Carl, who continued, "*I am a truck driver and I make long trips across the country. I understand that you live outside Chicago. I come through there from time to time. I am asking for a favor. We do not have to know each other, but my daughter really wants a sister. She is in middle school now, and I finally explained my past to her and told her about you. She wants to meet you. I could bring her to you. Would you be willing to meet her?*"

I did not know what to say. I just knew if I did not get off the phone soon, my boyfriend would have a conniption. I abruptly said, "*How did you get my number?*" and he replied, "*From your mother.*" I told him I was sorry and had to go. He said, "*I under-stand,*" and we hung up. I immediately called my mother. She said she had given my number to Carl. When I asked her why if he was not my father, and she said, "*He asked for it. He wanted to talk to you.*" I was beyond confused. With approximately 1,500 miles between us, I brushed it off and went to bed. It was not anything I could solve then anyway.

A number of weeks passed, and then a letter arrived. It was handwritten and included a school photo of a young girl. I did not know if she was my sister or not. In my mind, it was all a lie. I could not act like this young girl was my sister when I knew it to be a lie. I remember just staring at her picture for hours. She had a mole on her face, and so do I. She did look a bit like me. Could it be? No! I put the letter and picture in a shoebox in my closet. I suppressed it to my subconscious mind and went on with life ... for thirteen years.

It's funny how the brain works. Although we know our brains typically store our experiences into a form of memory, there are times when our brain protects us. Essentially, it walls off a memory of a traumatic experience for its own good. When our brains encounter an overwhelming fear or trauma, our brain can dissociate from it.

Recently, I met a beautiful, radiant woman in her late 60s. We were at a ladies' evening tea party at the home of a mutual friend. It was an intimate group, and we all offered our answers to the question, "Why not you?" The dialogue was amazing. Each woman explained what the question meant and how they worked through it. When it came to this older woman, she shared a very personal reflection.

It was clear that she understood why her life was the way that it was. She had repressed memories that came to the forefront of her consciousness only in recent years – memories that horrified her as she recalled sexual abuse from her father when she was very young. She told us how this had shaped her life, and how her brain had protected her until now. To her surprise, she was able to heal from it and now she truly lives, "Why not you?"

I spoke with her afterward one on one, and we exchanged contact information. In the weeks that followed, I was stunned to learn she had died. She was 68. I will never forget her. My witness of her radiance, her story, and the fact the she died just weeks later cannot be coincidence. Our Spirit comes through us – all of our senses, our thoughts, and our emotions. It is all there for us. It is our subconscious mind. I saw her gratitude in reflection. It was awe-inspiring. I believe we die from fully ripened love. When we see love to the point, our passing can only teach another how to love more deeply. I could feel her fully ripened love as she spoke from her heart to all of us. Now she is an Angel.

## Forgotten Memories

I have never felt closer to God than when I gave birth to my children. Welcoming a newborn child is an emotional time for any couple. There is an overwhelming amount of instinct that comes with parenting and the feeling that this helpless relies entirely on you. I remember thinking how brave it was to love fully. To love this much opened me up to even greater loss if something should ever go wrong. Yet, I knew better. For to love is better than to never have loved at all.

But wow! Everything paled in comparison to having a child. I was awestruck, so in love and sleep-deprived in a way I had never known before. In the weeks that followed, I witnessed the amazing father my husband was. Having never known a father myself, I was receiving first-hand the gift of what a "daddy" was through my eyes as a mother. I nursed my sons, and the early morning hours were so calm and peaceful. All I could hear was the ticking of a clock and the suckling sounds of an infant. My husband often lay sleeping nearby. I found myself not thinking at all. Who could possible think on no sleep? But I was *present* in the moment.

On one morning like this, a flood of memories suddenly came to me. I recalled walking through my childhood home with my best girlfriend. It was during my freshman year in high school. My mother stopped me as I walked through the kitchen and handed me the phone. I said, "Hello" and I heard in reply, "It is your daddy!

How are you?" I looked at my mother quizzically, and she smiled and kept talking to her friends who were visiting. Music was playing. I ended the call quickly, and I handed the phone back to my mother. It made no sense then, and it made no sense now.

The next memory to come back to me was a drive to Idaho with my grandmother – a woman I had not known. Yet I was suddenly introduced to her that same summer. I remember the beautiful mountains as we drove in a small Toyota truck from Montana to her home. It was an amazing adventure for me. I remembered staying in her home, but nothing else. My mother explained that Mildred "Millie" Cornwell wanted to spend time with me. Around the same time, I recalled staying with Sam and Marilyn in Spokane, Washington. Sam was Carl's brother. I know it was June and I had just been released from school, because I remember making a Father's Day gift for my stepfather at the time. I remembered Sam and Marilyn's home, a cabin in the woods that he built himself. I remember how tall Sam was. I could remember how radiant and loving Marilyn was. I even remembered dining with them on the river front in downtown Spokane and meeting their daughter.

As I sat there with my son in my arms, I thought, "How could I not have known all of this until now?" Soon after the memories came flooding back, I confided in someone who knew both my mother and myself for years. I posed my question and my reasoning. I wondered why my mother would send me to stay with someone who was not family. I felt an acute awareness now as I rocked my infant son, and I knew I would never do this to him. There had to be something more. At the same time, I processed all that my mother had told me to date. And I remembered more. She had told me that Carl was someone who did drugs and who went to prison. This information wrapped him in fear in my mind.

I knew I had questions, and I needed to get answers. I just was not so sure whether I wanted to open a can of worms and expose my family, my husband, and my son to this uncertain truth. I discussed it with my husband and he was supportive, but he did not see any reason to consider it. He encouraged me to trust that my mother had made the right decisions. I believed him; he was my rock. I decided he was right. At least, at the time, it felt right. Let us be honest though – it was just easier.

For years, I would think about this decision. I began feeling a form of guilt. I reflected on how my husband would feel if our son were not in his life –how that would hurt him so deeply that it could affect his life. I could never do that to him. In contrast, I thought about my firstborn son. He had not yet asked about my father, but I knew that day would come. Was I comfortable telling him that I knew this much and yet did nothing? I found that I was not okay with the answer. I would want to tell my son that I had done more.

I began looking online. I found Carl was living in Washington State. I pulled his public records and I saw that he had truly had some trouble with the law. In the years that followed, I began doing more research. I researched my ancestry and actually decided to evaluate whether this person was my father. I was able to trace the genealogy all the way back to the American Revolution in 1775. I was fascinated! Could that really be my family history?

I found the young girl who wanted to know her sister on Facebook®. For a year, I followed her feed. She was younger than me, of course, but she had to grow up fast. Her page was not private, so I could see she had two small children and was a young mother like my mother had been. Ironically, it looked like we had children the same age. My mind continued to process question after question as if to build a case for why I must pursue this.

Twenty-two years after the call I got that night when I was 18, I welcomed my second son home. It was as if I had a real conversation with God. Seven years had passed since the memories flooded in. On a soul level, I knew my second child was a miracle on his own. We had prayed for him for years, and when we were blessed to receive him, I knew I had work to do. I had to pay it forward. I found myself asking God for one year of solitude with my family before I embarked on a journey that I knew was necessary. I did not know what the truth was. I had come to terms with the fact that my current truth did not make sense. I prayed for strength. I prayed for forgiveness. I prayed for the protection of my intention as well as my relationship with my mother.

I wanted to find the truth for the benefit of that conversation I had 22 years earlier. I decided this was not about my mother. In fact, I did not want to trouble her with the emotion of it all, so I embarked on this quest alone. I decided to not speak with my mother about it until I knew the truth. Her story had always been *her* story and that answer was not going to change. I needed to find another path. Once upon a time, a young girl named Shibon asked to know me and I said no. I felt solely responsible for that, and only I could change that conversation. I accepted my decision and forgave myself for handling it the way I had. I had been so young, and to ask me to accept that my truth was somehow a lie or that my mother had lied to me just never seemed right. I knew she must have been protecting me. But why?

## The Quest

Another year came and went. My second son turned one. What a whirlwind year! You blink and another year is gone. I did not feel the time was up until Father's Day. On Father's Day 2017, alarm bells went off in my head. I thought, "Enough! It's time." I had made a pact with God. I got online that peaceful Sunday morning. I decided to send a direct message via Facebook® Messenger. I found the young woman I had been thinking about rather quickly. Shibon is a unique name after all. I found the words to write in a message I had been crafting in my head for eight years. I said a prayer and wrote this:

*"Hello! I have done a lot of thinking and reflecting, and I feel that you and I should connect. Your father reached out to me when I was 18, telling me you wanted a relationship with me. I was stunned and shocked as it meant I had been told a lie my whole life. I am married now, and I have two children. I think it is time that you and I get a paternity test to determine if we are in fact sisters. Can we connect? Graciously, Nicole (Cornwell) Martin."*

In just two hours, she replied, *"Oh my gosh! Yes, please!"* Our chat session began, and it was something I was not prepared for. The first blow came six hours later. It was a photo of me – my high school graduation portrait. Shibon had taken a picture with her phone and it was framed and hanging on a living room wall. I was stunned. I immediately asked how she got it. She explained that it was the one thing her dad had of me, and the only thing she had since she reached out to me as a young girl. Moments later she sent another message and told me her dad was sick. She wrote, *"I do not know if you know this, and maybe you will not care, but dad is sick with incurable cancer and was given the diagnosis three years ago. He is not doing too well, but he wanted to be sure I told you Happy Belated Birthday."* She was so patient and kind with me. She immediately expressed concern for me, and it felt like a warm hug from another human being who sought the answer to the same question.

Days came and went, and I leaned on my husband for support as the emotions were heavy even while I was compartmentalizing them. I had book launch parties and speaking engagements, and I certainly was not ready to discuss this matter with my young children. She sent sweet check-in messages. I had good intentions, and she understood that I was going to look into paternity tests despite the distance. The days turned into weeks, and a month passed. Shibon reached out by sending me two more photos – one of her and her brother, both very young. Then she sent a picture that her Aunt Lori had given her.

Another flood of shock overcame me. First, the girl in the picture was me at seven or eight years of age. I felt as if I were looking at a picture of my first son! I couldn't believe it. I don't have many photos from my childhood, and I never thought my son looked so much like me. It was undeniable. So, there was that thought coupled with the mention of *"Aunt Lori."* I wrote back, *"That last one you just sent looks a lot like my oldest son now. I have not forgotten about you. I have been so busy, but one of these days I will make it to Walgreen's to inquire about paternity tests. And who is Aunt Lori?"*

It was 10:30 on a weekend night. I was wondering who Aunt Lori was. I remembered a "Lori" from my early childhood – but she was my mother's friend. I even have a scar on my calf from when I burned myself on "Lori's" husband's motorcycle. Wait – could my mother's friend – the one I remembered so well – be my aunt? I was puzzled. Then another message came: "It is my dad's sister! It is so fun for me to see these. And no worries. My dad was also saying that the State of Montana should have paternity on file from when they tested him for child support. Would that be easier?"

As I read this message, I began to cry. How could this be? I immediately reached out for life support – I called my brother who, thankfully, is always up at night. I also messaged my best friend and soul sister back home. Both thankfully provided a much-needed perspective and I feel so fortunate to have been given the strength to grow through that moment. It did not matter if my mother received child support or not. What mattered was that I was her daughter and, as my best friend reminded me, I was always her child. Clearly, she was protecting me – but again, why?

I called the State in August. A case agent called back within hours and told me that I did have a case file, and she gave me the case number from a court order in Washington. I requested medical records – and then days turned into weeks. I spent those weeks learning more about this girl who claimed to be my sister. She worked in a medical office with varied hours including some weekends. I learned Shibon was funny. And yet, I was still so distant, and I had yet to pick up the phone and call her. I had opened myself to her, but I still did not open myself to her father.

Two more months passed, and I had an opportunity to meet her. I had a client engagement in Montana and hoped we could arrange to meet in December. Shibon agreed and said that her dad would like to see me as well. She reminded me he was sick. I expressed compassion for her, but I took it one step at a time as she and I both prayed for guidance. I was honest with her – I simply could not understand why my mother did not share this with me. Shibon began to share her sadness with me. She was watching her dad decline, and it was hard on her. I had to ponder … how awful could he be? She clearly loved him, but I needed more time. I wanted to see hard biological evidence before I invested more of me into it. I simply felt overwhelmed.

## The Gift

I learned Shibon's birthday was November 2. In the weeks preceding, I had a business connection as a guest on my online show, *HR in the Fast Lane*. He founded and ran a drug-testing and lab-testing firm. He provided drug testing for businesses, but only after having him on the show did I learn that he also provided more than 1,000 other tests, ranging from allergy testing to confidential STD tests.

I emailed him to ask for a favor, and within a day, I had an answer. He made a special accommodation for me to mail the testing materials, given that the suspected father was cooperative. I messaged her my "present" on her birthday. Shibon said it was the best gift she could ever receive.

Just before Thanksgiving, I took my test and sent it in, and she obtained her dad's test, and we waited. I received an email on Thanksgiving morning. My business connection wrote, "Happy Thanksgiving! I hope this gives you the answer you were hoping for!" I enjoyed Thanksgiving with my mother, my brother, and his family, and said nothing about the news. I just took the time to be present with the gifts before me and prayed with gratitude for the day. It was not until much later that day that I shared the email with my husband. We were traveling to our family cabin to celebrate with my in-laws. I read the email and shared the test results with my husband while we drove north and our children were sleeping. I read it without emotion. I said it without emotion. Yet, my whole body began to well up. I began to feel the sadness. Not in a sobbing, crying way. Rather, it felt like the final stage of grief. I was in acceptance. The report read, "The alleged father cannot be excluded as the biological father of the child. The probability of paternity is 99.99% as compared to an untested, unrelated man of the Caucasian population. A prior probability of 0.5 was assumed." And there in black and white was the truth. Carl Cloyce Cornwell was my father.

I accepted this truth but still I was processing how to take it forward. I gave myself some time to be with it. I sent my sister a message, "It is official. We are sisters. I got the lab results yesterday. What is your email? I will send the DNA report. It seems I will need to make a trip to Washington, maybe in the fall of 2018." She told our father, and she said he teared up and smiled despite being in pain from chemotherapy. She let me know he said, "I always knew it!"

I knew I needed to make this trip, but I wanted my husband to travel with me. He and I discussed the possibility of a trip the following year. I was still nursing my second son, and we both agreed I would make the initial trip without the children. So, it would have to wait. Meanwhile, I was still planning a business trip to Montana, but I had yet to confirm the logistics if I were to pair it up with a personal day into the weekend that followed. The days that followed were a flurry of messages between us. A flood of stories, information, birthdays, contact information, pictures. It was like we were cramming a lifetime into a week of chatting around both of our busy schedules as working mothers.

## Life Goes On And Time Runs Out

It was the final day of November. I was working and attending an evening event in the city. My sister texted me midday asking if I was available. I did not get back to her until my train ride home, around 10:00 pm. She said our father had fallen, and she had to help him up. She was deeply concerned. I finally asked all the questions we had never discussed. How was he? She said his diagnosis was lung cancer and while he had been living with this for three years, he had originally been given just three months. I asked if he was a smoker. She said he had quit in 2010 but he worked in chemical plants. We began to discuss the possibility of a video call, but he was so medicated that he slept most of the day. We had a great deal of back-and-forth that week trying to make it happen. Meanwhile, he was put on a respirator. She was hoping to make a call happen, and I remained on standby. I had so many commitments, but I stole a date night with my love, and then it was *The Nutcracker*, and the preparations for the retreat I would be facilitating. It was now December. She sent a message: "I wish more than anything that he could see your face just once. The doctor told us to go home. We have 24 to 72 hours. He is going to pass." We both tried so hard to make a video call, but he never really came to again.

I was enjoying the HRBoost holiday gathering at a comedy venue downtown, and I did not review my messages until afterward. It was 10:31p.m. on December 2 when I called my sister for the first time. Six months of virtual communications between us had come to this moment. Our father was dying, and she was by his side. Neither of us could change that fact. She was so devastated, and all I could do was talk her through my peace. I let her know I was there for her, and that I would travel to be with her for the funeral. I let her know I was sorry that she had lost her dad. Personally, I felt so at peace. I explained to her that maybe he was ready to let go. He was in so much pain and knowing that she and I were connected and building our relationship brought him joy. I did not feel the need to talk to him or the need to see him. I felt the need to be there for her. I told her this was the only thing he ever asked of me. He never asked to know me. He asked me to know *her*. I let her know my gift is learning what a good person he became, regardless of his youth. I had decided he was a different man when he had her, and by losing me early in his life by the choice of my mother, I could see he learned to be a great dad to her, and that is beautiful.

The time had come to talk to my mother. She and I have opposite schedules, and I wanted to really sit down with her and explain my intentions and everything that led to this moment. I made the time to see her the day before flying out west. As I sat with her, I knew I had one task. I needed her to know that she was the best mom ever, and that I loved her unconditionally. I wanted her to know that no matter what her truth was, I accepted it and hold nothing against her whatsoever. I cannot imagine having a child at 19 and providing the life I had, so she has no judgment from me. As I began to explain the memories that came back to me and the realization that nothing made sense, she began telling me her truth. This time was different, however. While I wish I had heard it earlier, I felt why it was good that I heard it in that moment and not a moment earlier. She explained that she was with my father for a year, and it was great. Then he got into drugs – and not small stuff. Heavy drugs like heroin. She said it scared her, and she left him. She met Leonard and they fell in love. She had been with Leonard for months when Carl came to the house in a drug-induced rage. I know that stimulants can change a person – in fact, it can change your brain chemistry forever, and another severe downside is that they cause paranoia, aggression, and even delusional behavior. Needless to say, I could accept that this could occur. My mother explained that he became possessive and, in her mind, he kidnapped her. He took her back to his home and locked her in his bedroom. In her mind, he raped her and terrorized her for a full day before someone came and let her out. She pressed charges. He was incarcerated, and she went back to Leonard. She learned she was pregnant, and when I was born blond, she believed I was Leonard's. She explained that if I ever wondered how she left men so easily it was because she learned never to return to the ones she had already broken up with. Carl taught her never to go back. Leonard died, and my mother went back to Carl, and we lived with him during my first year of life.

I was suddenly able to see her view. All this time, I'd wondered if she even knew the answer and, in that moment, I knew her truth was what she needed to believe. I knew her well enough to know that she would never want to believe I was conceived from rape, or rather not from an act of love. She regards her relationship with Carl as something other than love. She has strong sentiments for me to be created from love. I can perceive that, despite his erratic and crazy aggressive behavior, he in fact loved my mother. I have learned that many people love in the only ways they know how to. It may not be the pure love as love is intended in 1 Corinthians 13.

As she finished her story, I thanked her. I hugged her. It felt amazing! It was in that moment I realized that maybe I was healing this for her. All these years, she has been a healer, and I felt I never could be a healer, yet here I was sending healing messages to her, my Father in heaven, my new sister and now to you. I realized that the irony was that I had the power all along to heal this. I thank God for the strength to see the choice and the ability to see it through. There were many times along the journey that I could have continued to take the easy path. It had become my responsibility but, more important, it was my opportunity. I handed her the report and said, "Mom, Carl really is my father. He died yesterday. I am going to meet my sister and brother, and I would like us to pray together for this trip and for my father's soul." We did exactly that. I left and began the journey to meet my sister.

What a gift to be paid to work in my home state. I had arranged to rent a car on Friday after work and drive to Washington through the Idaho pass. It was breathtaking. I arrived in Spokane late that evening, and before the day was done, I had met my sister, her children, her mother, and her other siblings. It was surreal. As I sat in the home of my father, it struck me as oddly like the home of my mother. There were certain elements that let me see and feel the ways that he and my mother could have come together at one point in time. At the same time, I learned so much about my sister's life and those of her step-sisters that I began to feel how different my life would have been if it were not for my mother.

## Be The Light

We all have the power to choose. Often, we choose imperfectly, but God made us to be imperfect. Often, we fall, but we can choose to get back up. Often, we see darkness and feel pain, but we can choose to see the light. I want nothing more than for you to feel the joy and delight in God's love. It is all around us. Becoming deeply rooted in our own spiritual growth is a personal and intimate process.

Life is not meant to be rushed. However long it takes to feel the whole pieces of ourselves, it is as it should be. We all seek love, but we do not all seek God. I have found that by seeking my joy and purpose through *presence*, I can seek to heal and love in new ways. I seek God in every corner of every room. In my breath and in the breeze. I believe we all can be the light that burns radiance within each of our God-given souls. Uncover your beauty, go on a quest, and uncover your story!

I pray that by taking this personal journey with me, you have found new ways to overcome challenges, believe that you deserve to be not just happy, but *joyful*. I pray you found new sources of gratitude. I pray you have new ways to see the beauty in your soul's journey and live a life that affirms your God-given gifts for the service of others. I pray you overcome any unwarranted fears and feel the grace within you – a mindful and conscious *presence*. Each day, ask yourself, "How can I grow in a capacity to love more fully, more deeply, and more overtly?" You will surely see you have all the power within you.

*"Presence is more than just being Present."*

–ANONYMOUS

PRESENCE TOOLS 7

——————— UNCOVER YOUR STORY ———————

*I pray you have come to a place of empowerment. You can write your story and, at every point, you can change the elements to realize the happy ending you desire. Follow your truth and honor your intuition. Like any story, your life has many chapters and, within each, you plot the story. To realize your story, consider these eight plot definitions. I used this Eight-Point Story Arc[10] to help me share my story with you.*

**Only you can uncover and write your story the way you choose.**

**Stasis**

This is the "everyday life" in which the story is set. Think of your life – your status quo. It could be where you began or where you are right now.

**Trigger**

This is something beyond your control.

**The Quest**

The trigger results in a quest – an unpleasant trigger (losing a job) might involve a quest to return to the status quo; a pleasant trigger means a quest to maintain or increase the new pleasant state.

## Surprise

This stage involves not one but several elements, and takes up most of the middle of your story. "Surprise" could include pleasant events, but more often means obstacles, complications, conflict, and trouble.

Nigel Watts, the creator the *Eight-Point Story Arc,*[11] emphasizes that surprises should not be too random or too predictable – they need to be unexpected but plausible. The reader has to think, "I should have seen that coming!"

## Critical Choice

At some stage, you are faced with a crucial decision, a critical choice. This is often when we find out what we are truly made of. Our true character is revealed at moments of high stress. Watts stresses that this has to be a decision by the character to take a particular path – not just something that happens by chance.

## Climax

Your critical choice will reach a point of climax, the highest peak of tension, in your story.

## Reversal

The reversal should be the consequence of the critical choice and the climax, and it should change the anticipated outcome of your story.

Your story reversals should be inevitable and probable. Nothing should happen for no reason; changes in status should not fall out of the sky. The story should unfold as life unfolds: relentlessly, implacably, and plausibly.

## Resolution

The resolution is a return to a fresh stasis – one where you have opted to change the outcome. You are wiser and enlightened.

*(You can always start off a new story, a sequel, with another trigger because life goes on …)*

when you write the story of your life don't let anyone else hold the pen.

*"Consider it pure joy, my brothers and sisters, whenever you face trials of many kinds, because you know that the testing of your faith produces perseverance."*

–JAMES 1:2-3

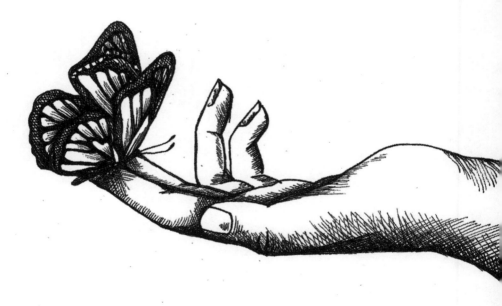

# *About the Author*

## Nicole Martin

Nicole has been recognized by numerous organizations for her commitment to professional excellence and her community. These include the Daily Herald Business Ledger Influential Women in Business award, a Women of Distinction honoree and most  recently she was named a 2016 Enterprising Women of the Year Champion by *Enterprising Women Magazine*. As a highly regarded and sought-after expert, her knowledge and advice have been featured in newspapers and magazines throughout the country. She has been featured or quoted include Forbes.com, the *Daily Herald Business Ledger* and *Fast Company*.

A self-professed "country girl in disguise," Nicole Martin grew up in Montana. The small-town setting, where everyone knows you and greets you on the street, was the foundation for her dedication to transparency and accountability in all ways, both personal and professional. Nicole was fortunate to have a great mentor early in life: her mom. A highly spiritual woman, Nicole's mother raised her with the philosophy of being happy and sovereign with God. She ingrained in her the belief that every person is special and unique and that we are each capable of pursuing our passions as they are the calling from God.

Nicole leads as CEO and founder of her own successful consulting firm. As a sought-after speaker and author, she gives all grace back to God. God makes it all possible and only through this has she come to know her joy and purpose can be expressed in service through her work.

Her expertise provides more to an organization than just a corporate culture boost or a good office vibe. She links human capital directly to profitability time and time again — and she's got the analytics path charts and the logic models to prove it. All people deserve joy and purpose through their work and workplace ministry can be found in truly seeing one another and caring enough to believe in shared leadership.

Nicole resides in a northern suburb of Chicago with her husband, Brian, and their two sons. To learn more, visit *www. nicolemartin.live* or *www.hrboost.com* or follow Nicole Martin on Twitter @HRBoostLLC

# About the Presence Tools

The Tool sections throughout this book are intended to be self-guided and practical. These same tools mirror the process Nicole has taken to source Joy and Purpose more fully. These tools are meant to build on one another and herein you have a whole toolbox ready for you to fall back on when you are feeling out of balance and in need of some self-love.

# About the Contributors

Christina A. Zorbas, content contributions include tools featured in Presence Tool sections 1, 2, and 3. As a Holistic Health Practitioner (HHP) trained through the Holistic Health Institute (CA), she has successfully owned her private practice for over 40 years. She incorporates a variety of holistic therapies, advanced massage techniques, and energy work into her practice for effective and natural healing.

Kristina Nennig, Illustrator. Her content contributions include the sketches found throughout this book. Kristina Nennig fell in love with art ever since she could hold a pencil. She has been won best of show for her illustrations in multiple competitions across Chicagoland. Kristina attended Iowa State University where she received a Bachelor Degree in Graphic Design. She specialized in Illustration, Graphic Design, and loves anything creative. If you would like to see more of her work visit *KristinaNennig.com*.

# References

1   "Rose Quartz Meanings and Uses." Crystal Vaults, 10ADAD, 2017, *www.crystalvaults.com/crystal-encyclopedia/rose-quartz*.

2   Red Flags, A Safe Place, *www.asafeplaceforhelp.org/content/red-flags.ree*

3   Negi, Radha. "Where did the concept of chakras originate?" Where did the concept of chakras originate? - Quora, 25 May 2017, *www.quora.com/Where-did-the-concept-of-chakras-originate*.

4   Wauters, Ambika. Life changes: with the energy of the chakras. Crossing Press, 1999.

## Principle 4

5   Young-Sowers, Meredith. Wisdom Bowls: Overcoming Fear and Coming Home to Your Authentic Self. Stillpoint Publishing, 2002.

6   Upchurch, Catherine, editor. Little Rock Catholic Study Bible. Liturgical Press, Collegeville, Minnesota, 2011. James 2:18

## Principle 5

7   "Fear – The Cheapest Room to Live in the House." EthicsDaily.com, 11 May 2012, *www.ethicsdaily.com/fear-the-cheapest-room-to-live-in-the-house-cms-19590*

8   Kabat-Zinn, Jon. Mindfulness Meditation for Everyday Life. Piatkus, 2001.

9   Jackie's Website Make It Happen Journal, JJR Marketing, 2014, *jackie-camacho.com/MakeitHappenJournal*.

## Principles 7

10   Watts, Nigel. Writing a Novel. Hodder Headline, 2006. "Eight-Point Story Arc"